THE
RUSSIAN WRITER'S
DAUGHTER

D1557802

THE
RUSSIAN WRITER'S
DAUGHTER

STORIES OF GROWING UP AMERICAN

LYDIA S. ROSNER

MAYAPPLE PRESS 2012

Published by   MAYAPPLE PRESS
                362 Chestnut Hill Rd.
                Woodstock, NY 12498
                www.mayapplepress.com

ISBN 978-1-936419-10-4

Library of Congress Control Number: 2012932819

ACKNOWLEDGEMENTS

A special thanks to Harriet Sobol and everyone in her wonderful group of devoted writers whose encouragement and helpful comments played such an important part in my completing this book.

A special thanks to Rona Robinson and Barbara Roberts, whose first readings were so helpful, and of course to my wonderful children, Beth, Marianne, Josh and Garth, for all their love and encouragement.

Cover photo by Abraham Sokol and newspaper article originally published in *Novaya Russkaya Slova*. Cover designed by Marianne Klimchuk and Judith Kerman. Book designed and typeset by Amee Schmidt with titles in Futura and text in Calisto MT. Author photo courtesy of Beth Giokas Rosner.

CONTENTS

This book is for
Aaron
Niki
Noah
Sasha
—the future

Much as I own I owe
The passers of the past
Because their to and fro
Has cut the road to last,
I owe them more today
Because they've gone away

—Robert Frost, "Closed for Good"

THE TRUNK

"What are you doing?" Mama asked. Papa was sitting at the kitchen table in front of the large steamer trunk with a pile of brown A&P shopping bags on the chair next to him. The black leather trunk was almost as tall as I was. The brass, rounded-corner hinges were particularly beautiful, I always thought. This was the steamer trunk that Mama had packed in Kishenev for her journey to America, when she was just seventeen. She, her sister and her father had traveled in comfort as evidenced by the trunk that Mama and Papa kept in their bedroom, part decoration and part utility storage.

I had stopped by to have afternoon tea with Mama and Papa, traveling uptown by subway from the apartment where Jonny and I lived on 23rd Street. I had always loved that trunk. On the left side of the opening, there was a metal rail from which hung graceful wooden hangers, and on the other side were three small drawers and two deep ones, with shiny steel pulls. The top of the trunk folded back onto itself so that it could serve as a dressing table.

"I'm going to reline it," Papa said. "I'm going to use these bags to recover the inside."

Papa was wonderful with his hands. He could make belts, pocketbooks, book linings, and paper the insides of wooden chests. These skills eventually allowed him to make a living when his hopes for a writing career diminished.

"But why are you going to reline the trunk now?" Mama asked, looking at me as if I could provide the answer. She had just come into the apartment carrying several bags of groceries that she put down on top of the stove.

"And maybe if you want to do this you could do it tomorrow or on the weekend. I have to make dinner and we should eat," she said. "Riva and Friegan are coming for tea." Riva, my aunt, was almost like a second mother to me. Although she lived with Aunt Olga, a third sister, she was an independent woman, and Mr. Friegan was her current boyfriend.

"Ma, I'm going to have to leave after dinner, OK?"

She continued her unpacking. "Sure, go ahead. You should be there when Jonny gets home."

Mama put the cake box on top of the refrigerator next to the radio and started unpacking cans from the grocery bag and storing them in the bottom of the tall kitchen cabinet on the other side of the room. She walked back and forth and around Papa, who had gotten up to push the trunk into Alex's room.

"I don't know why you want to change the lining. It's beautiful as it is," said Mama. She looked at the trunk. "I really like what you did already. So why change it again?"

The inside of the trunk was a colorful assemblage of United States maps, available free at every gas station. Papa had pasted them down in such a way that no writing showed. There was not a bump or lump anywhere. The muted reds and greens and yellows of states and counties, intersected by green roadways and blue rivers, created an elegant lining that looked just like the expensive luggage on display in the windows of the better Fifth Avenue leather stores. "I like the way it looks. Why would you even think about redoing it?" she asked again. Papa noticeably paled.

"Alex called. From Broadway," he said.

Mama had started to pull out pots from the cabinet that was on the right side of the large stove. She placed a frying pan on the grate and turned the knob. Then she took a match from the large metal matchbox holder hanging on the wall and lit the burner. She and Papa had turned off the gas to the stove pilot light. They didn't want to worry in case the flame went out and the gas kept on escaping, especially at night.

She turned to Papa, who was now back in his chair, the trunk out of sight. "So why did Alex call? What did he want?"

"He said he was in the phone booth on the corner in front of the Bermans' stationery store and the *New York Post* headline says that Jack Sobel was just arrested."

"Oh my God," said Mama. "Oh my." She walked away from the stove and sat down at the table. "Oh my," she said again. She looked at Papa. "But why?"

"Alex said the paper says Jack is a Soviet spy and they have been watching him and his friends Myra and Jack Albin. He said it's all over the papers, *The Post*, the *News* and the *Mirror*. He said that their pictures were on the front page of the *Times*. He's bringing the papers. It says that they were part of a spy ring acting for the Soviets. It's all over the news and he said people are talking about it in the store." He sighed. "They've been watching them for ten years, Alex said the *Times* says."

He put his chin in his hand, and I could see how upset he was. "I don't know what they're going to do with them—and what about Larry? I mean what happens to a thirteen year-old boy when his parents are arrested? And what do they tell him? And what is this all about?"

Jack Sobel's son Larry was my brother's friend and lived next door in 210 Riverside Drive. The boys would visit back and forth, play ball on the Riverside Drive playgrounds, and I knew that my brother loved the magnificent set of Lionel Trains that circled Larry's large bedroom.

It was 1957. Since 1950, when Joseph McCarthy had proclaimed that the State Department was full of Communists and Communist sympathizers, there was fear in the air. And for my parents, who belonged to unions, who spoke Russian and who had sent me to IWO *International Worker's Order* camps, now listed on the Attorney General's list, it was a time not just of fear but of terror. Safely ensconced in my new marriage, my life had become removed from that of my parents and brother. But now, sitting there in my parents' kitchen, I suddenly felt drawn back to their world of emotions that I had always considered overreaction.

"Alex's number, our phone number, is in their phone book, I'm sure," Papa continued. "God knows what they're going to think about us. We weren't even friends. Just Alex and Larry. Just because they played trains together on rainy days and visited back and forth, but who knows what can come of that."

Papa had never trusted government. Ever since he had been forced to leave his own Odessa, a city that he continued to love, he had mentally kept a suitcase packed, ready for another expulsion. Mama, never fearful, tried to calm Papa down. "It's just boys playing. Who can think anything more than that? Please calm down. They don't want us, why would they? When is he coming home? And what has this to do with the trunk?"

"But still, maps, here in the house. And what if they come here. What do I do with my writings and my books?"

We heard the door open, and Chief, our dog, came running down the hall into the kitchen, followed by my brother. Alex was breathless and sweaty. " I ran all the way home. What about Larry? What will they do with him? Who will take care of him? Where are they taking his parents?" He rushed on. "The Bermans in the stationery store said the FBI had been in there asking questions."

He sat down at the table across from Papa. I looked at him. He was red from the run home and yet somehow he also looked pale. I thought about the news.

"Oh wow," I said, half to myself. "That tan car parked on the corner of West End Avenue. I always passed it whenever I walked to Broadway. For years. And they were always there. Just four men. Just sitting in it. Just sitting. Not doing anything. Not even talking to each other. I always thought it so strange but then I never said anything because I thought I was just silly and suspicious, like I was during the war when I always thought people were signaling to each other from their apartment windows. But I always noticed it. They must have been FBI, watching their comings and goings. Their house. Their car."

Papa stood up slowly. He walked out of the kitchen, taking the newspapers with him. Alex went into his room to do his homework. I sat in my usual spot next to the stove and watched Mama cook dinner.

"What a tragedy this is. If what the papers say is true, Larry will be without a family, and he'll forever know that his parents were spies. How could they do that? I really didn't know the Sobels that well but they seemed like such normal people," Mama said. "I'd see her at the Daitch Butter Store on Broadway. She always got the sweet butter in such large chunks. And she was so polite to Mrs. Mahoney at the counter, always asking about her husband and family. How could she be a spy? It just doesn't make any sense."

I nodded, not knowing what to make of the whole thing.

After we finished our dinner and while Papa was doing the dishes, Riva and her friend Mr. Friegan arrived. After Papa told her about the excitement and Mama talked about how Larry was going to be alone, I left my parents' apartment and took the subway downtown to resume my newly married existence, my American dream.

On Sunday, when Jonny and I came for dinner, the trunk was back in Mama and Papa's bedroom. The shelves had been replaced. The drawers were back in their sequence. The wooden hangers hung against a drab brown-bag background. The drawer fronts sported brown under their shiny steel pulls. And there was an acrid smell in the house, as if paper had been burned, and the file of Papa's writing in the living room was half as large as it had been.

MAKING MARZIPAN

How strange that after all of these years the memory is so clear.

Seven little people crowded around a miniature table, blending and kneading the green dough. Hovering over them a brown haired woman, her plaid dirndl skirt reaching to swollen ankles encased in thick stockings. She is wearing a flowered apron, bibbed and lacy, covering her ample bosom and white cotton wide sleeved shirt. She has the face of a benevolent saint and the demeanor of one as well. Her blond hair, arranged in thick braids, glows around her head. She pulls me into an enveloping embrace against her generous frame. "*Daragaya*, dearest," she whispers.

We were making marzipan in the little Russian kindergarten in basement of the Russian Orthodox Cathedral on Amsterdam Avenue. Although my parents left Russia on the eve of the Revolution, after pogroms had ransacked Jewish communities, they sought Russian affiliation here in their new country.

The white stucco basement walls were striated with crenulated cement columns that rose through the floor to the church itself. There they continued up to the nave. I loved watching shards of sunlight pierce the stained glass windows and play on the dark wooden pews whenever we went there.

But of that day, I remember that ghoul-like green color of the marzipan and how I kneaded and patted, pushing the dough one way then another. Making first an orange. Then a pear. A cigar. A pancake. Another orange. A pear. I was trying not to get dough on the apron my mother sent to school with me that covered my short blue skirt and capped sleeved white blouse.

My best friend Helen, standing next to me, was busily tasting her creations. Her portion of dough kept getting smaller and smaller. "*Lenushka, daragaya*," Mam'selle implored. "Helen dear," she said in

Russian, the language we all spoke, "you will not have anything to take home to your *Babushka*." Helen's face began to scrunch. Her eyes filled with tears.

"Oh *Lenushka*, don't cry dear," and Mam'selle handed her another blob. "Try to keep it together my sweet," she said in her melodious Russian.

I was almost five, and Russian was my only language. Around me, in the apartment house where we lived, on 144th Street, were people who spoke English, French and German. But my parents, part of a Russian *intelligentsia* community of emigrants, Russian Orthodox and Jewish atheists, had made the decision to raise their American born daughter in what they believed was a superior culture. One that did not have boogie music or embarrassing vocalizations sung in voices that obviously had not been classically trained. And part of that plan was to send me to the Russian nursery.

I loved my kindergarten. I loved the warmth of the church base-ment. I loved Mam'selle. I loved that the Papas swirling by in their long black priestly garb always had time to smile at me or utter a "*Dobre Den*, good day," to us little people.

The smell of marzipan mingled with the smell of the decorated Christmas tree, whose lights sparkled in the corner of the basement, its candle shaped lights, full of colored liquid with dancing bubbles rising to the top. I loved the pageantry of the Russian holidays. The church smelling of incense. The voices of the choir, operatic and full. The colorful statues of saints and the old people who would come to light candles and to sit quietly on those long wooden pews.

The marzipan was for the Christmas festival. We would leave some and take some home. It was the last day of class and we were coming back that evening for our play. I was to be a butterfly, and my mother had spent nights at the sewing machine. She had fashioned my wings from re-bent clothes hangers, and my skirt was made of toile. But the best part, and I still have the picture in my childhood album, was the crown she made to top my braids, which were wound twice around my head and anchored with copper colored hair pins. The crown was made of sequins and had two shiny antennas that moved when I walked.

In my memory, Mam'selle takes my apple shaped marzipan and wraps it in cellophane. All seven of us crowd around her and she walks us up the stairs. Her girth makes our journey a slow ascent. She opens the tall wooden church doors, the arch above them reaching into the heavens. We exit, clutching on to her, and I see my mother smiling. With her is *Babushka*, Helen's grandmother.

We run down the steps with our marzipan in our hands. "Merry Christmas," we say in Russian unison, "Here, this is for you."

FISH ON FRIDAYS

Helen leaned over and whispered in my ear, hardly silenced by her hand cupping her mouth. "It's Friday," she said. Mrs. Nelson smiled and pretended she did not to hear that announcement. Helen repeated in her excited whisper. "It's Friday." I turned my head, causing my braids to swing, and nodded.

"All right, everyone. Please put your crayons back into the jars." We began to gather the fat crayons. Mrs. Nelson walked around the room making sure that all fifteen of us were working together. She seemed to tower over the three round wooden tables and us in our miniature chairs. "Now write your name on your drawings." Her voice soft., she leaned over to help one of the children with his backward *N*. As she collected our papers, I looked at Helen and smiled.

"Now you can go to your cubbies and hang up your aprons," added Mrs. Nelson.

"No running or pushing please."

Helen, called *Lyena* in Russian, was my best friend. Only recently have I begun to wonder what happened to her mother. But then it was Helen, *Babushka*—her grandmother—and Kola, her father. We had gone to Russian kindergarten together and spent almost every day in each other's company. We'd started public school together, too. Although I remember my friend clearly, P.S. 186 on 145th Street eludes my memory. I know that I was there, as was she, but somehow I cannot recall much else. Not the halls. Not the classrooms. They seem to meld into that generic New York City public school template. Lots of staircases shrouded by metal bars that separated the *UP* from the *DOWN*, tiled floors polished to a slippery finish, wooden tables in lower grades and desks with brass inkwells. Cement steps on the outside and cement play yards for recess. Green walls and oak doors. Auditoriums whose enormous doors slid on metal rails so that classroom space could be opened to house the entire school for our weekly assemblies.

At P.S. 186 I entered an English-speaking world of admirable teachers who had to contend with the new America. Children who spoke Russian, Polish, French, German and Hungarian. All new to this country. All running from a European world that was going up in flames. 1939. 1940. Only the Negro kids, as we knew them then, were American. But they too were refugees in their own country at that time. So *Lyena* and I belonged together. Our families had apartments with rear windows across from each other, her building facing 143rd Street and mine 144th. And we visited back and forth, having tea parties, playing with paper dolls and giggling. My father, Abram (*Bam*), and hers, Kola, had strung a wire between our two apartments over the open courtyard and attached paper cups to the ends. They were incredibly proud of their engineering skills; their creation of this sophisticated device for their daughters' enjoyment.

Helen and I spoke Russian to each other on this "telephone," but usually the message was unclear, so we had to resort to the old way, shouting across the courtyard and sharing our thoughts with all six floors of neighbors whose windows also faced that yard. On rainy days, or if her *babushka* and my mother were busy, we could play with our dolls without even being in the same room, talking in exaggerated high-pitched voices, pretending to be characters other than ourselves. Her windows had white thick cotton curtains, starched and with lace edges. Ours were sheer so she could see me whenever she wanted to.

It seemed that our families were intertwined. Winters, we all sat in one house or the other. But in those few summers that we still lived across from each other, Kola would take us to tranquil places where we would picnic: Stony Brook, where we took out a rowboat; Rocky Point, where we walked to the very mossy end and looked down at the breaking waves. Kola with his Seagram Seven, Papa with his ice water. I have scant memories of those days. Snapshots interspersed with memories of a happy childhood. Of being adored.

But it was Friday, and that meant fish. Mama and *Babushka* would be waiting for us, and we would go to Bickford's for lunch, as we did every Friday. That was what the excitement in class was all about. Eating out was a rare thrill. Mama was a wonderful cook, and she spent a lot of time at the stove. Years later she'd say that she hated cooking. I think that was because she had to do it every day. If we went out, it was for tea, never dinner.

"Please come over for tea, *daragaya,* dear," a friend would say. Tea was the ceremonial visit. Always a tablecloth. Always cloth napkins. And pastry. Tea in the afternoon. Tea in the evening. "Come at eight, for tea." And tea had lots of cakes, cookies, loads of sugar and conversation. I have no memories of dinner invitations except for special occasions. Birthdays were important. New Years even more so.

Helen and I followed Miss Nelson and the rest of the children from our class, who followed the second grade, who were behind the third, down the front stairs for that daily school ritual called *dismissal.* A word that had a regal sound and a celebratory character.

At the bottom of the steps, I saw Mama and *Babushka* engrossed in a conversation with Mercedes' mother and two other women. They looked solemn and intent. We knew, without even hearing what they were saying, that they were talking grown-up talk not about Bickford's or lunch but The War. I heard them say "Poland" and "German invasion" and "Hitler." And I heard Mama say that there were no letters coming from Europe and that things didn't look good at all. *Babushka's* English was not very fluent but she was certainly holding her own in this solemn conversation. The Hungarian woman seemed teary, and I heard the lady whose accent I knew was German say, "Oh, my family, my family."

"Mama," I pleaded in Russian. "It's Friday. Let's go." I got her attention and a big hug. Helen pulled at her grandmother's long skirt. *Babushka*, looking very much the Russian immigrant, bun pinned to the back of her head, flowered shawl on her shoulders, put her arm around her granddaughter.

"*Daragaya,* dear, we're going, we're going," she patted her granddaughter's head. "Bad things are happening, and we have to talk about them, but I know you are hungry." I looked at my friend, so small standing next to round *Babushka*. Helen's beautiful, I thought, with her blond hair and skin that I now know is called "peaches and cream."

Bickford's Cafeteria had tiny black and white tiles on the floor and metal-rimmed laminate tables. Behind the counter, men in white aprons tended the steam table and dished out the food. The line was not too long, and the four of us joined the other mothers, the men who came there every day for a place to meet, and the storekeepers from the market across the street. We waited impatiently with our trays. It was Friday, and that meant fishcakes and mashed potatoes. How delicious. Just what we were waiting for and what Friday was all about. But somehow the mood seemed somber.

Babushka looked at Helen, her smile betraying her emotion. "Finish it all, *daragaya*. Eat. Eat. Remember the poor children in Europe. They are all starving."

A PIANO LESSON

Aunt Olga's apartment, on 137th Street, was bright and light, with large windows facing the street. Oriental rugs, collected during years of living abroad, illuminated the floors. Music filled the air. Aunt Olga, prim and specific and very direct, was the matriarch of the family. Her older sister Biba had died in Canada, leaving behind four children and a husband. Olga brought one of those children, Bess, now a college student, to New York to live with her and Uncle Shura in their wonderful sunny apartment, near Riverside Drive and down the hill from Broadway.

Mama, Alex, and I were sitting at the white metal-topped kitchen table watching Olga make cherry *verenikas* and listening to beautiful music coming from the front room. Olga, efficient as always, had created a production line in the middle of her kitchen. There was a glazed ceramic bowl covered with a damp cloth that held dough, a Pyrex dish for flour and a bowl of cherry filling that she had boiled on her stove earlier that day. At the edge of the table were two wood rolling pins and the stack of damp dishtowels that she used to cover the *verenikas* to keep them from hardening. There was a pot of boiling water on the stove. Olga stood while she shaped and filled the small circles of dough. We talked over the sounds of the piano being played in another room. I was sorry that Bess was not home. Although I was still in elementary school, I always loved seeing her.

Olga, her hands covered with flour, would roll out some dough and then, with an inverted glass, cut it into rounds. She'd put some of the cherry filling on half of the round, cover it with the other half and pinch the edges with her fingers. She would then turn back the damp towel covering a flat pan just far enough to place a finished *verenika* on it. On the tall radiator, next to the stove, there was a stack of eight pans, each covered with a damp towel. Some of the towels had red stripes on the borders. Some had blue checks. All were immaculate, as was everything in Olga's house.

Alex kept on reaching into the bowl of cherries, and his fingers had acquired a red tint. Olga, looking but never being stern, said in her precise Russian, "*Shurik*, dear, stop. You want to take some home to Papa, don't you? Leave that, and you can lick the bowl when I'm finished. And I'm going to make some really small ones, just for you. Let me get you some cookies and a glass of milk. Just wait."

She wiped her hands on her apron and walked to the tall refrigerator on the other side of the kitchen. The glass into which she poured the milk had daisies on it. It wasn't like the thin glasses, inserted into metal holders, that she used to serve tea to Mama and me.

The sounds of Czerny exercises, rapid arpeggios and booming bass notes, exploded from the baby grand in the front room, down the hall from the kitchen. We stopped talking and just listened when Rachmaninoff's "Piano Concerto No. 3" replaced the Czerny. I had heard it practiced throughout the winter and now there was not a hesitation or a repeat. The sounds were rich and perfect. The piano, tuned to perfection every six months, had a magical tone, but it was the hands that played it that brought out such a glorious sound.

Olga always had music students living with her. The large, sunny, front room with its grand piano brought from Germany and the location of the apartment just walking distance from Julliard were ideal for those whose lives revolved around a musical future. The students who lived there were always practicing: Chopin, Beethoven, Tchaikovsky, sonatas, concertos, arpeggios, scales and more scales. Music was the constant in my Aunt Olga's apartment; life there always had a musical accompaniment. When Uncle Shura was home he'd sit in the living room, legs crossed, cigarette in its holder, newspaper in his hand and pretend to read when I knew he was just really listening, enjoying the music in his life. I loved it when he was home because he would always have something interesting to show me—the barometer he had brought from Germany, a salve his friend was trying to patent that could cure rashes and sores, a picture he had salvaged from the basement that he knew was worth some money. But on that morning, he was at work in the patent firm that he had founded in Germany and recreated here in America.

"Oh. Olga. Will you have any of those wonderful *verenikas* for me? I can already smell them. I knew you were going to make them when I saw you set out the pans." The young man who entered the kitchen had a head of curly blond hair, much like my brother's. His charm warmed the room, and both my mother and Aunt Olga smiled at him. He wore a short-sleeved blue plaid cotton shirt and corduroy tan trousers.

"Of course, Eugene," my aunt smiled at him. "I always make some for you." Eugene, satisfied that he would be fed, turned to us.

"Oh. Hi, Alex. Hello, Lydia. Going to have your lesson later?" He glanced at me.

Eugene Istomin was one of my Aunt Olga's favorites. He was a musical genius who had started performing at age 5 and by 12 was a student at The Curtis Institute. Years later he married Pablo Casals' daughter, but just then he was simply a roomer in my aunt's apartment and my current "other" piano teacher. My regular teacher had a school of her own, and her students performed at concerts to which parents and relatives came. Eugene was extra. His indulgence, teaching a non-musical-prodigy, was probably generated by the fact that he received a rent reduction for tolerating me as his student.

"Yes, I guess I'm ready when you are." I started to get up, smoothing my plaid skirt.

"Let me get something to eat first," Eugene said as he went toward the refrigerator. I sat down again, happy to wait.

He did not appear to look forward to our hour of struggle. And I, my piano career a dream of my mother, whose world of classical music was supposed to be acknowledged by my participation, did not look forward to the struggle either.

Eugene's appetite was not quickly satisfied. He lounged at the table, his feet crossed at the ankles, his manner studied, aristocratic. He had taken out the sour cream and found some chopped up vegetables. He mixed them together slowly and added some pepper. My Aunt Olga poured him a glass of tea and, taking some crackers from the cabinet, served them to him. Eugene ate slowly, relishing each bite. The conversation lagged around him.

Finally, my impatience to get it over with got the best of me.

"I'm ready when you are, Eugene."

He stood up and put his dishes in the sink.

"OK," he said. "Com'on."

We walked down the hall to his room, and I sat down on the piano bench. Eugene pulled over a chair and sat next to me. "Put your music on the music stand, and I'll start the metronome."

"OK, let's start with scales," he said, leaning back and looking out the window. C, C sharp, D, D sharp, on I went. My fingers flew over the keys. I then started on the octaves. Up and down the keyboard, double scales. The piano sounded wonderful. And I, after five years of lessons, was able to master my assigned task well.

"You know," Eugene said looking at me, "after all, when I think about it, your hands are wasted on you, really wasted." He did not look pleased. "You could do so much more if you cared. Look at that spread. Really! If you cared and practiced you could really be somebody."

"I'm already somebody," I answered, hating him, his aloof approach to me, his know-it-all attitude. I even hated the fact that my childish crush on this tall blond piano maven was not acknowledged. And I didn't like having to play the piano, either.

As I continued with the scales, not really concentrating, I could hear Olga and my mother chatting in the kitchen. They were enjoying themselves, laughing. I could hear the cars on Riverside Drive. I could hear the whole world going by while I was stuck there, in that bright, sunny, front room playing the piano with this handsome young teacher whom I had begun to dislike.

I wished that I cared that I had the hands of a pianist. I wished that playing the piano did not seem so European. I knew that I would never be the pianist that my mother hoped for, and I did not want to participate in her dream any longer. I wished that I knew how to be disobedient.

Three years later another Russian piano teacher, giving me private lessons in her Broadway apartment, picked up my hand and looked disdainfully at my bitten nails. "What boy would ever want to hold such a hand?" she snarled.

I made the choice. Boys, nails, and not piano. And a disappointed mother.

THE BALL

Hundreds of tiny bulbs sparkled, layers of them on the enormous gilt chandeliers. Crystal droplets reflected the many-colored gowns below, turning the ceiling itself into a multicolored extravaganza. I thought that the ballroom of the hotel looked like a fairyland. We walked down the wide, thickly carpeted steps onto the polished oak floor. I was nine and Papa's date. Actually, I was his pride. Mama had stayed home with Alex, my little brother, who was a only few months old and still nursing.

Gowned women from the Tolstoy Society, the refuge of *White Russians,* as they were called, who spoke French and pretended that they had been part of the Russian Royal Court, slipped about air-kissing each other on the cheek, clucking at me in my braids and organza dress, complementing Papa on his last published story in *Novaya Ruskoya Slova*, the New York Russian newspaper, and tossing their boas. Their hair was uniformly blonde, usually upswept and adorned with jeweled combs, their faces powdered and rouged, their noses upturned. Ample bosoms slipped from tight, outdated dresses that belonged to another place, another era. Their smiles were contagious and a bit strained. I thought they looked enchanting.

Across the river, in Valley Cottage, New Jersey, Countess Alexandra Tolstoy, daughter and secretary to the novelist Leo Tolstoy, had founded the Tolstoy Society. Throughout my childhood my parents spoke with some derision of these White Russians who pretended that they were better than the rest of us. I had heard countless stories about her "farm" and the old Russians who populated it. These were the lost souls who had fled Russia after the Monarchy was overthrown and whose memories of their days in the Court became more elaborate with the passing years.

And although the Countess did help resettle innumerable new emigrants from the old Russia, now the Soviet Union, my parents always questioned her motives, believing her interest lay in associating herself with their pretentious heritage, royal bearing, and the *intellegentsia* label for her own enhancement.

Papa was invited to the Ball because he was a member of the Proletarian Writers and Artists Society. Only many years later did I realize that the company that he kept (Mayakovsky, Burluik, the various futurists, avant-garde artists and members of the Russian–America press) made him an elite in the Countess's eyes. The rarified atmosphere at the Barbizon, where depressed and overdressed self-proclaimed and dispossessed members of the Russian royal court preened and pretended, was fun to observe. Papa's courtly demeanor and elegant style made me, hanging on to his arm, proud, and yet even at that early age, I detected that this world, this European manner, was not what I wanted for myself.

The two of us wandered about the ballroom, visiting with those sitting at tables adorned with starched white tablecloths and arrangements of carnations and roses. The conversations around us were of worldly things, the terrible things that were happening in their home country, the inability of those who had fled to France to gain entrance to America, and the changes in their own lives. Around us the dancers spun to the waltzes, and the orchestra played on and on. Papa was stopped many times as we circled the room. The conversation then was usually about his last play or his Writer's Circle with its famous ex-pats.

I was hugged by a large woman. She was sitting spread-kneed at a small table at the edge of the ballroom.

"Here, come sit with me for a while," she enticed me. "Have some tea and some of this wonderful Sacher Torte with me while everyone is dancing about." Papa indicated that I could sit. He moved over toward the dance floor.

I knew that her name was Tamara and that she lived uptown. I'd seen her many times before in the neighborhood bakery, Le Petit Paris, where we would go to buy French pastries for dessert. There she wore a long apron and Mama always said that she waited on the customers as if she were doing them a favor.

"Come, *daragaya*, sit while I talk to you. I have so many stories. Oh so many to tell. The past is the past, but I can tell you a little about everyone here. And not just of their past. Sometimes I think I know too much, just too much about everyone's present, too. It is the present that is often so hard to take, to explain. The past we had no control over. Or maybe we have no control over our present, too." She leaned toward me. I tried not to show her that I wanted to move away a little. The smell of her gardenia cologne was overpowering.

"See that woman over there?" She pointed at an elegant woman with a haughty demeanor, dressed in a long brown velvet dress. The white fur boa draped around her neck and hanging down her back looked to me like an unhealthy animal. "That one fanning herself so quickly, in that brown dress. She claims that she grew up in the Palace."

I had heard about the Palace before. "Oh, the Palace!" Mama would exclaim. "There isn't one single Russian here it seems who doesn't claim to have lived in, worked in, or been in, the Palace." And according to Mama, it seemed that there was not one non-Jewish immigrant who did not claim either a royal background or at the least some personal contact with the Czar, the Czarina, or the Royal Court.

But Tamara had her tales to tell. "That's Marianna Pavlovskya, daughter of the Czarina's second maidservant. She grew up right with the Czar's family. They even let her sit with the children's tutor. But, poor dear, she lost everything when they had to run. And her husband was killed. She was lucky that she had a ticket to Paris for her summer vacation. And there she starved all alone until finally someone took pity on her and brought her here." She shifted closer to me and put her arm around me.

"But I'll tell you now, all she does is put on airs. Like she is nobility itself. Look at her."

Instead, I looked around for Papa. He was talking to a white-haired man dressed in a velvet jacket. On his lapel there was some sort of a satin emblem. Next to it were several gold medals. He clicked his heels and bowed, and then he made his way in our direction. Papa, with a smile on his face, followed.

"This is my daughter. *Leda*, Lydia." The man smiled at me and kissed Tamara on both cheeks. "Your Papa tells me that you are a writer too," he said.

I stood up. "Papa, can we go?"

Papa put his arm on my shoulder. "Lydia has published stories in the *Novaya Ruskoya Slova*. In Russian. She is here to look into Russian Society," his Odessa humor coming to the fore.

"But she is still only nine. So we have to be leaving. It's past her bedtime." He bowed with courtly grace.

I could see that Tamara and the gentleman in the velvet jacket were not ready to give Papa up yet. But he and I walked back up the thickly carpeted steps, across the lobby of the Barbizon and to the Subway.

"They're all fakes," he said.

THE MOVE

I often wonder whether it was the rock, the roomer, the concessions, or what Papa called "the tide" that brought us from 136th to 93rd Street.

The rock.

When I woke up that morning I could hear Papa muttering to himself about "damn this, and damn that." As I opened my door the little bell that Papa had installed over my doorframe jangled. He had screwed it onto the white molding and centered it so that each time my door opened the bell jingled. I knew that they were worried that the woman to whom they had rented a room when I was ten, one of many roomers we had during my childhood, might come unhinged. The bell was to protect me from her should she choose to visit during the night. Papa had said he had to figure out a way to get her out of there.

"She told me yesterday morning that she had been thrown out by her family. If I'd known that I'd never have let her move in. And the references she gave me said she was a lovely person, but now that she's been here for two weeks, I can tell that there is something crazy about her," Papa said.

That little bell jangled whenever I came or went, and before the move, I actually had begun to enjoy the sound. The *crazy lady* was never part of my life, but I did know that Papa had been calling her parents and telling them that she had to find another place to live.

I walked into my brother Alex's room where Papa, dressed for work, was pushing broken glass into a metal dustpan. He was wearing his navy blue suit, and red birds cavorted on his tie. Alex, standing in his crib, was quietly watching as Papa brushed the glass carefully into the dustpan and emptied it into the green metal garbage can that sat in the middle of the bedroom floor. Papa moved around the room, bending down and straightening up again. One piece of glass caught the morning sunlight. I thought it sparkled like a diamond.

Papa took off his suit jacket and put it on the chair in the corner. Using his hand he tried to gather the jagged shards of glass that had scattered all over the room. Some of the pieces were on the oak floor near the kitchen door. Mama was standing there just looking upset.

There was a large rock on the floor between the double windows, one of which was broken. I stood there looking at the mess and wondered how I had slept through the noise of the rock breaking the glass. Alex, who had just learned to pull himself up on the crib railing, sat down with a thump, put his thumb in his mouth and started babbling his feed-me-breakfast tune.

"Be careful," Mama said to Papa as she walked over to pick up my brother. She turned to me and added, "*Leda*, be careful. Don't walk barefoot in here. There's glass all over and probably even little pieces out in the hall. Go put on your slippers." She bent down to pick up a shard of glass. "Better still, go get dressed. You have school, and I still have to make lunch for you."

"What happened?" I asked.

"I … nothing. Nothing to worry about. Somehow … Oh, someone threw something and it came in through the glass." She turned toward me. "Go. Go. Don't worry about it. Get dressed for school. It's late and you need to get ready. It's nothing. There's nothing to worry about."

Mama did not look as if it was nothing to worry about. Her face was red. She lifted Alex out of the crib, still clutching his favorite blue blanket, and with him straddling her hip, walked into the kitchen and put him into his high chair. Turning to the stove, she lit the fire under the pan of Cream of Wheat, my breakfast.

"*Bam*," she said, using my father's nickname, "maybe you should take the pail down to the basement and empty it. I don't want the glass here." She looked even redder. "I'll vacuum the floor after I take Lydia to school." She removed the pot of cereal from the fire and spooned it into my Cinderella bowl. She put it in front of me and handed me the honey and my spoon with the Prince on its handle.

My father took his jacket from the chair. He took his hat from the hall closet and put it on. It was a black felt fedora, and I thought it made him look very handsome. Putting his wool coat over his arm, he picked up the pail and started out the door. He turned back to give me a kiss, and putting his arm around my mother, whispered something in her ear and left.

"Mama, how did the glass get broken? Did someone throw a rock into the window?" I asked.

"Don't worry about it," she said. "Go get dressed or you'll be late." Always secrets, I thought.

That evening at dinner, I tried to talk about the rock and the glass, but neither Mama nor Papa wanted to answer my questions. Mama said something quietly to Papa in Yiddish, and then they started to talk about the war. Papa and Mama talked about how the Americans were finally landing in Great Britain. Papa said that maybe that would shorten the War. There was war talk every evening at dinner, and I was always shushed when there was news coming from the little radio on top of the refrigerator.

No mention was made about the events of the morning, and I didn't ask. I excused myself to go to my room to do my homework, but I could hear Mama and Papa talking Yiddish, the language of secrets. I tried to figure out at least the gist of what they were talking about, but since I really couldn't understand much Yiddish, I kept losing the thread. I could tell that they were talking about things other than the war. I went to sleep wondering what was going on.

The concessions.

Our apartment on 136th Street had four bedrooms. One for Mama and Papa, one for Alex, one for me. The fourth was always rented to "roomers." The strange woman, because of whom Papa installed the bell, did not talk much and kept to herself. Since she did not have what Mama called "kitchen privileges," she was rarely seen and was not part of our lives.

But there were concessions everywhere. It was 1942. There was a draft. We lived in a ration book world, and all Americans had been asked to abandon luxuries. There were more apartments than renters, and so landlords offered rent-free months called *concessions*, where for two months or even as long as six months, tenants did not have to pay. That summer when Mama and I were living in the country and Papa came for weekends, I'd collected milkweed pods for life preservers for our Navy. And I always carefully took the tin foil off of my chewing gum wrappers and added it to the large ball of foil that Mama kept in the kitchen. And I tried to remember that "loose lips sink ships," although I was not quite sure what that meant.

We had just moved a year ago, from 144th Street to 136th Street, and I had been transferred from P.S. 186 on 145th Street to P.S. 192 on 138th Street, right near City College. And now I knew that Mama and Papa were talking about moving again. Further downtown.

I could interpret parts of the Yiddish conversation that Mama and Papa had at the kitchen table every evening after I went to my room to do my homework and after Alex had been put to bed. From my room next to the kitchen, I could hear them, always that mixture of Russian and Yiddish, talking about the war, the economy and recently, the rock. It wasn't that I understood every word, but somehow, straining to hear, I could get the essence of the conversation.

Recently they talked about how, if they rented out two or even three rooms, it would cover the whole rent. And night after night, Mama would tell Papa about the apartments she had visited and how there were concessions all over and lots of apartments to choose from.

"And we need to keep ahead of the tide," Papa said one evening. "Even if we can't afford it, the tide is moving down."

The tide.

The Hudson River was just two blocks away from our apartment, across Broadway and Riverside Drive. And we spent lots of time in Riverside Park enjoying the playgrounds and the river breezes. So I thought I understood about the river. And we had learned about tides in school. But I wondered: how did an apartment near the river have anything to do with the tide? Why did Papa think that the tide was moving down? Down where? I wondered. I tried to understand. Maybe it was the translation that was confusing. But no, Papa had said the word *tide* in English. What did that have to do with us? Or with concessions? Why did Papa feel it so important to keep ahead of the tide? I tried to understand but couldn't.

Each morning Mama put Alex into his black carriage with its large white wheels and walked with me to P.S. 192. She avoided the groups of men who congregated in front of the red brick building across the street from our house. They seemed to be there whenever we went out, and they never sat. They were always just standing around. Laughing. Poking at each other. Sometimes, when we walked out of our building, Mama walked faster than usual and put her hand over mine on the carriage handle, hurrying me along.

"*Leda*, hold on to the carriage and don't look at those people."

"But why?" I asked. I was too old for things like this.

"Because you need to mind your own business, and we have nothing in common with them. They just hang out and don't work and anyway we're late, so walk quickly."

I glanced across the street. One of the men had a brown paper bag in his hand and lifted it to his mouth. "Hey sweetie, ho'ya'doing?"

Mama rushed me along.

"Come, you'll be late for school. Just walk."

When I came home from school that day, Papa and Mama were sitting at the kitchen table. I could see that Papa had stopped at Le Petit Paris, the French bakery on Broadway and 138th Street. Papa, although always slim, loved pastries and often brought them home on the way from the subway, "*for tea*" as he said. But it was early for him to be home. He was still wearing his shirt and tie, and Mama had on a grey wool skirt and high heels. I wondered why.

"Sit down for a moment with us," Papa said.

Mama poured me a glass of milk and, taking a plate from the cabinet, put on it a marzipan fruit shaped pastry, my favorite.

"So *Lyduce*," his pet nickname for me. "What do you think about moving to a new apartment?"

I really hadn't thought about it at all. "I don't know. Why?"

"It's right near the river, and there's a beautiful park with a statue of Joan of Arc right there," Papa continued.

Mama added, "And you'll go to a wonderful school, P.S. 93. And you'll have a room with your own bathroom right near the kitchen. And Alex will have his own room too."

"So, what do you think?" Papa asked me the question, but I could see that he'd already made up his mind and certainly there was no decision for me to make. Not that I had a particular opinion. Mama and Papa circumscribed my life; I was living in their world. What did I know about moving? As long as they were with me, the rest was irrelevant.

I don't remember anything about the move, except that the crazy woman's parents were there at the same time as the moving truck.

We left her behind when we moved to the seven-room apartment on 93rd Street that overlooked the Hudson River. This neighborhood, on the west side of Broadway, was primarily Jewish. And the Irish kids who lived between Broadway and Central Park West listened to their parents and went to church. Refugees from Germany and Austria also resided here, and so the schools served a population that, until the '50s, spoke a variety of European languages as well as English. Here, there was predictability and decorum.

But I still don't know exactly what prompted our move—the rock, the crazy roomer, the concessions, or the tide—neighborhoods slowly changing from uptown, down.

A SCHOOL PICNIC

By the time I was in the second half of fourth grade, class 4B, I was allowed to walk to school by myself. I had been allowed to skip 4A for reasons now unknown but which resulted in my never really knowing the eight times table and always having a January graduation. But on that particular sunny June morning I was sitting at the kitchen table with my dish of Farina and glass of milk before me, watching Mama pack my lunch: sandwich, apple, thermos of chocolate milk, and cookies.

Mama stood at the counter space on the right side of the stove. She was wearing an ironed, maroon, striped housedress and her hair was neat and combed back into its usual braided bun. Mama never appeared without her hair combed, and she always reminded me that if your hair is neat, your table free of dishes and papers, and your bed is made, you are ready to face the day.

Mama had grown up a much-loved darling child, the last of 16 born to her mother and father. Eight had lived and her mother had died in childbirth. I think Mama always carried somewhere in her heart the knowledge that her coming into the world had removed her mother from it. Her father had had to hire a wet nurse, a woman who had just given birth to her own child, to come in and feed Mama.

Mama had four older sisters who helped raise her, along with a nursemaid and servants who took care of the house. Pictures of her as a young woman show her as beautiful, sylph-like and leggy, with long hair down her back—hair long enough to sit on. I knew that in Kishinev, where she was born, she lived in a house with land enough that a synagogue was built on the part that her father had donated to the Jewish community.

Mama always spoke about her father in adoring tones. He was a man who was able to raise a family without a wife and to successfully bring them to adulthood, educated, with a love of music and poetry and art. He had protected them all during the pogroms. But when Kishinev was annexed by Romania in 1917, with the two oldest girls married and in their own homes and the sons already in America, he brought the two youngest, Riva and Rose, my mother, to America with him. Mama always said with pride that they came as ticketed passengers and were not funneled through Ellis Island like less fortunate immigrants. Her shipboard trunk bears witness to the fact that she brought an extensive wardrobe with her.

So Mama was very conscious of appearances and of how to maintain them. She never went out without wearing a dress and three-inch heels, hair and lipstick in place and a leather handbag acquired with the help of, or as a gift from, my father. She was conscious of how I looked as well.

"Mama, you're pulling," I cried. "It hurts." Our conversation was, as always, in Russian. Even though by the time I was born Mama and Papa were fluent in English, our private language, the language of home and family, was always Russian.

My hair, long enough to sit on, was combed daily. Mama first made two little braids at the top and then braided them into the long thick plaits that hug way down my back. The ribbons at the end always matched my outfit for the day.

"Shush," she said, bending down to plant a kiss on my head.

"You've got the class picnic today, and you want to look nice. Just be still for a minute longer." Mama was sitting, and I was standing in front of her waiting for the end of this daily ritual. She combed each section as it got shorter, tucking it into the braid that was now below my waist.

"Now what color ribbon?" she asked. "Blue to match your shorts or yellow to match the flowers in your blouse?"

"Can you use two ribbons together? Blue and yellow? It's a picnic, and I think that would look pretty. OK?" It was a warm sunny day, and I was looking forward to being in the park with my friends.

Mama walked into the bedroom, got the two ribbons and finished my braids. Then she handed me my lunch box and, hugging me to her, escorted me down the long corridor to the door. The usual admonitions: "Be careful crossing the street. Look both ways. And don't talk to anyone you don't know." A big hug and a long kiss, and I was off. Mama blew a kiss through the small glass window as the elevator door was closing.

The day was beautiful. A June perfection. Sun, warm and comforting. A slight breeze was coming off the river, just enough to keep the day from being hot. A perfect picnic day, I thought.

I walked to West End Avenue and looked both ways. There were others going in the same direction. I found my friends Rosalie Schulman, dressed in a navy skirt and white blouse, and Peter Rosenblatt, in his usual grey slacks. Peter often came home for lunch with me, because his parents, both doctors, were never home, and because my mother's table always had room for another.

"Is your class going on the picnic too?" I asked Rosalie. Peter was in my class, so I knew he was coming.

"Yes," she said, "It's a school picnic. Every class is going."

I had just moved to 93rd Street that year, and P.S. 93 was my new school. I liked the friends that I had made there. Many of the children had parents who had been born overseas, in Germany, Austria. Refugees, we called them. Looking back I realize that, other than the Irish kids who lived east of Broadway, my world was an immigrant world. It wasn't until years later that I could sort out the class distinctions between the Central Park West and West End Avenue families and those who lived on the side streets.

We walked up the stone steps and through the wooden doors. I smiled at the hall monitor, a grown-up sixth grader, standing just inside. Peter and I went up the stairs to our classroom after saying good-bye to Rosalie.

Mrs. Gottlieb was at the door of the room greeting us as we arrived. She looked at me, dressed in my new flowered blouse and the blue shorts that I was wearing for the first time, for this special day, for this picnic.

"Lydia," she said. "Lydia. Come up here." She looked cross. "This isn't summer camp you know. You can't wear shorts to school. Shorts are not allowed in school, and I can't let you come to the picnic if you wear them."

"But ..." I sputtered.

"No ifs-ands-or-buts," said Mrs. Gottlieb, turning away from me. "Now if you hurry you can go home and change. Go ahead, hurry up. We can't wait for you, so you have to run."

I ran from the school across Broadway and West End Avenue to my house. When I rang the doorbell Mama came to the door with Alex on her hip. I was perspiring, and my braid had begun to come undone. "What's the matter?" she asked.

"I have to change. I can't wear shorts. I have to put on a skirt. I have to hurry," I blurted out and started to cry. "I don't want to go back."

"*Lydushka*, go ahead and change, dear, and don't cry," Mama said, also looking unhappy. "I don't know why she sent you back. What's wrong with shorts? You look so pretty. Go and put on that plaid skirt that you wore yesterday."

By the time I got back to the classroom, everyone was lined up ready to go downstairs and walk to the park. I found my friend Peter, and together we walked down the stairs, down the block, across West End Avenue and into Riverside Park. The sun was shining, but it was no longer warm and comforting, and it was no longer a wonderful day for a picnic.

PAPA'S CITY

I held Papa's hand. "Don't touch that banister," he admonished me. "Hold on to me. Everyone touches that, and it's full of germs." I also wasn't allowed to eat pretzels from street vendors, whom Papa called "dirty people." I was 13 years old. We were going down the stairs at the 96th Street subway station on the downtown side. People on the right going in, people on the left coming out, New York style. Papa nodded at a woman coming up. She was wearing a hat with a tall beige feather and a coat that was made of some sort of brown tweed. I thought it was too warm for a coat. Her stockings were baggy around her thick ankles. The dark seams curved toward her outer leg.

"Good morning, Mrs. Maloney." Papa slowed down.

"And a top of the morn' to you too, Mr. Sokol. What are you do-ing going down to the subway with a pair of pants tucked under your arm?" She smiled at him. "And is that just in case you'll need them later?" She chuckled at me. "Hello, dear. You heading downtown with your dad, now, are you?"

I knew Mrs. Maloney because she worked in the Daitch Butter and Egg store on the corner of 93rd Street. She always had a piece of halvah for me when we walked in and sometimes gave me a lump of butter from the big tub when she was carving out the pound piece for Mama. And when Chief, our dog, was with us, she allowed him to put one paw on the counter edge so that she could give him a piece of farmer cheese. I smiled at her as we continued down the stairs. "Bye, Mrs. Maloney," I said.

Papa and I were taking the IRT to 34th Street, and then we would walk to Ninth Avenue. Things were cheaper on Ninth Avenue, Mama and Papa always said. It was a spring Saturday morning, and we were going to shop for groceries and visit some of the merchants whom Papa had gotten to know from the years when he was a regular in that neighborhood, back when he worked for the City of New York.

He had been appointed as a Social Worker in the Welfare Department, a new agency created in 1939 as part of the Roosevelt Works Progress Administration. In those days he walked the streets of New York visiting families in financial need. His love of walking the streets of his beloved city hadn't ceased even though he no longer worked there, a failure that Mama really never got over. His love of life, of dancing, and his stubborn refusal to take the test that would have grandfathered him into the Civil Service system was to forever change the direction of our lives, or so Mama said years later.

"Hello, Alphonse," Papa said to the blind man who stood on the sidewalk shaking his metal cup and tapping his white cane. "How goes it today? Making a living?"

"Ah, Mr. Sokol. Not so bad. Not so bad. It's good to hear your voice. Who've you got with you this morning? Your little girl?"

I looked at the man Papa was talking to. He was wearing a slightly wrinkled gray striped suit, a navy shirt and boldly flowered tie. His glasses were round and very dark, with metal earpieces. I tried to see his eyes but couldn't.

"Yes," Papa said. "We're going to do our weekly shopping. Walking over to Ninth Avenue. It was good seeing you again, Alphonse. Take care of yourself. See you soon."

Alphonse turned toward the woman who had dropped a dime into his cup.

"Thank you, ma'am."

We continued our walk toward Ninth Avenue. I held on to Papa's right hand since he had the pants still tucked under his left.

"So, *Lyduce*, I want to tell you a story," Papa said, laughing. "I walked into the movies last week, the Stoddard on Broadway, to see *Song of Russia,* and guess who was sitting there with a woman and two children. Alphonse. And he was looking at the screen and watching the movie. I've known him for years, and he makes a pretty good living standing there downtown on the street looking blind. A real faker." Papa chuckled. "What a life."

When we got to Ninth Avenue, we walked into the cafeteria on the corner. "How about a nice piece of cake and some milk?" Papa asked.

We took our trays and, sliding them on the metal rails, moved down until we came to the cake section. Papa put a piece of frosted chocolate cake and a glass of milk on my tray and took cake and tea for himself. As we made our way toward the cashier's counter, I saw

Papa notice a sad looking man sitting in the corner. "Stay here for a minute," he said as he went back and took another piece of cake and another cup of tea. He paid and, carrying the tray toward the back corner of the cafeteria, walked toward the sad looking man. I walked slowly behind him.

"Victor. How are you?" He put the cake and tea in front of the man. "Listen, Victor, I'm glad you came. I brought you those pants I promised you. I hope they fit. I think they will. " He put the pants on the sad man's lap.

"Thank you. You're a good man, Abe. You take care of yourself now. And enjoy that pretty little daughter you have there. Why don't you go take her to sit by the window where it's light."

Papa and I walked to the front. He shook his head. "There but for the grace of God go I," Papa said. I didn't think Papa believed in God. But he always said that whenever he helped anyone.

Papa and I finished our tea and cake and continued down Ninth. The day was warm and sunny, and many of the storekeepers were outside visiting with each other or arranging merchandise on the sidewalk displays. Every so often someone nodded to Papa or called out a greeting. I held on to Papa's hand while we walked, feeling proud.

By the time our shopping bags were full, we'd visited all the people Papa knew on Ninth Avenue. Dominic, standing next to his vegetable bins, made sure that Papa got the freshest black radishes and beets. At the Italian market, Joe filled a bottle with green oil and made sure the cover was tight before handing it to Papa. Marie chose the rye bread with the most caraway seeds from the back of the tray and gave me a cookie with pine nuts to munch on. All of the merchants we visited had a kind word for Papa, and he'd ask about their families and how their children were doing in school.

On 27th Street, Papa stopped in front of a small store window covered with colorful fabric. You couldn't see into the store at all. There was a glass globe revolving on the sill, and tassels were hanging from the top of the window frame. Cards and stars and a picture of a woman with a turban were pasted to the inside of the window. A large metal sign that said *Palms read, Fortunes told, See your future* on both sides stood on the sidewalk right in front of the door, from which a colorful beaded curtain hung.

The woman standing just outside of the entrance was round and smiling. Her dark hair was pulled up in a lazy bun, and curly wisps escaped and fluttered around her painted face. Red lipstick surrounded her lip line and her cheeks were painted to show round circles of matching color. Black pencil around her very dark eyes and many skirts layered on top of each other defined her gypsy bearing. Her off-the-shoulder blouse was black and lacy, and the bracelets on her arms jangled whenever she moved.

"Abe. Good morning. How's life treating you? I guess OK from the look of all those groceries. Looks like you bought up the street." When she smiled at him I noticed a large gold tooth. It shone, reflecting the sun. She put her hand on his elbow and started to move us inside. "That's a load of food for you to carry home. But you're a big strong man so I'm sure you'll manage."

"And how are you, Gitana? How was business this week?"

Inside the walls were covered with thick fabrics, rugs, tassels and mirrored cloth. The air felt thick and heavy and smelled sweet. I wanted to go back outside.

"I think I made my rent this month, Abe. It's good that the weather is letting people out of their houses. And maybe there's more money around."

We were just inside the door. I tugged on Papa's hand.

"Papa, let's go," I said.

"Sweetheart, come sit down and let me read your palm. I'll tell you about your future." She put her hand on my shoulder and tried to guide me farther inside. Her skirts brushed against my bare legs, and I tried to move away. "Come, sit down over here and I'll do the cards. Or maybe you'd like me to read the tea-leaves. Which would you like better, dear? Sit and we'll see all about you."

"Let Gitana read your palm," Papa said.

'No!" I was emphatic. "No, I don't want to. Let's go."

"Why not?" Papa asked. "She'll tell you your future."

"NO."

"OK *Lyduce*. Gitana, I guess we're going. See you soon. See you soon."

As we walked back toward the subway, I could still smell the incense stuck in my nose and feel her touch on my arm. There was something that disturbed me about that woman. I didn't know what.

"I don't want anyone to tell me my future," I said to Papa.

"Ah, I don't believe that stuff. It's just bunk. But don't be upset about it."

"Yes, " I said. "But how does she know all that stuff?"

And I thought, no fat, over made-up fake of a gypsy was going to put a spell on me so that I wouldn't have the future I wanted.

When we got home Mama asked about our day. "It was fun," I said. "We saw so many of Papa's friends. And he gave those pants to a man who looked so sad. And there was this fat gypsy lady who wanted to tell me my future but I didn't want that at all."

Mama started to empty the bags of groceries. She smiled at me. "Just do your homework and study hard, and you will make your own future. Your dreams will come true."

I walked into my room and thought about all the people that Papa knew and wondered about the lives that they lived. I wondered if they had families who loved them. And children.

And I was proud Papa was able to be part of so many different colorful worlds. But I knew in the very core of my being that while those worlds would be part of my past, never would they be part of my future.

THE INVITATION

I was sitting in my usual place, tucked between the kitchen table and the stove. The plates and silverware were drying in the rack on the left side of the sink. Papa, whose refrain was always, "I'll do the dishes; I have a system," had already done them and taken Chief for his nightly walk to Broadway. As always, he promised that he'd stop at Cake Masters and bring home something sweet to have with our tea. It was a Friday and I already had my hair up in rollers, ready for bed. Tomorrow was movie day on the West Side, and my high school friends and I were going to the Loews' 83rd to see *The Ten Commandments*. Charlton Heston did not rate the same adulation as Van Johnson, but we thought he was quite OK.

Chief came running into the kitchen. And then I heard Papa's voice.

"Trafeim's here," he called. I could hear their footsteps in our long hall. They had to walk past four bedrooms, round a corner and then come past the living room. I didn't like sitting there with curlers in my hair, but by the time I could get up he and Trafeim were entering the kitchen.

"Hello," I smiled. "I'm going to my room to do homework."

"Don't go. It's OK." Papa said with a knowing look. He took off his coat. He was wearing his usual black shirt and black string tie.

Trafeim hung his navy pea jacket, the black shiny buttons etched with the Red Star, on the back of the kitchen chair nearest the hall door.

"Let me hang up your coat," Papa said reaching for it. "You'll be more comfortable."

He said that because Mama did not like coats on chair backs. She also believed that only rude guests put their hats on the table.

"It's OK," Trafeim said in Russian. "I'll leave it here. I'm comfortable always in your house, Abram. I'll just leave it here behind me, if you don't mind." He smiled and set his square shape on the chair opposite me. I looked at his hands. They were large, almost paw-like and looked chapped. A middle finger seemed to be missing a nail. And there was an anchor tattooed on his right hand.

Papa took off his own coat and walked back down the hall to the closet. I heard him drop the wooden hanger, grunt, and then close the closet door.

"Rosa," he called again. "Trafeim's here. He brought halvah and cake. And Russian Kvass even though he knows *we* don't drink. He says we should save it for company." I started to get up again, but Papa motioned for me to remain sitting. "I'll put on the tea."

Several months ago, Papa had come home and told us that he'd invited someone new for dinner. Apparently Trafeim had picked up Papa, or vice versa on the 42nd Street IRT subway platform.

"You don't mind, Rosa, do you? We've plenty of borscht, and I bought a large rye bread. Sweet butter, bread, sour cream, soup. A good meal," he'd said that day. "It was really nice to find this guy there. We hit it off. Nice man. Lonesome. At first, before he opened his mouth, I thought he was maybe an American merchant marine, but then I heard him and saw the red stars on his pea jacket."

From then on, whenever Trafeim's ship docked in New York, he'd call from a phone booth near the port and garner a dinner invitation. And here he was again, after dinner, for tea.

"So, Trafeim, where have you been?" Papa walked over to the sink and filled the teakettle. "We haven't seen you in months." He called again, "Rosa, Trafeim's here."

"How are you?" Papa asked Trafeim. "How have you been? Tell me all about your last adventure at sea." Papa lit the burner with a match and sat down next to me.

"Hello, hello. What goes?" Mama came out of Alex's room. "I was just putting Alex to sleep. Please talk quietly. I finally got him to turn off the light. Trafeim, how are you?" Pulling open the silverware drawer, which was always tricky because of all the coats of paint, Mama took out spoons and forks.

"I'll set." She started moving things around on the table. "*Leda*, please get the napkins." My kitchen duties were few. Napkins, bringing the dishes to the sink to be washed. And sitting near the stove watching Mama cook or Papa wash dishes while engaging in conversation.

Mama took the pink glass plates that we used for company out of the cabinet and put them on the table. She still had her apron on, but as always, her brown hair was neatly pulled back in a bun. She was wearing high heels, because Papa was six foot one and she was just five feet. Papa always liked her in heels.

"It's windy out, yes? You both look so red." It was always windy on 93rd Street, with the wind blowing from the river over the statue of Joan of Arc standing on a rise between Riverside Drive and the park.

She looked at Papa. "Your face is very red." She walked over and rearranged his sparse hair. "Trafeim's face, well, he's a sailor so … It's always red, no?" she smiled. "Always red." She opened the bottle of Kvass and, taking a glass out of the cabinet, poured him a mighty amount.

Trafeim took off his watch cap and shoved it into the pocket of his jacket, which was so long that it almost touched the floor.

"Red face, red nose, red country. What can I say? Oh. I brought you the new volume of Pushkin," Trafeim reached into his jacket pocket and brought out a small package. "I thought you'd enjoy this."

On his last visit he and Mama had gotten into a long conversation about Russian poets, and he'd recited a long Lermontov poem from memory. "We all had to learn Lermontov in *gymnasium*, high school," Mama had said after that visit. "But Trafeim seems well educated for a merchant seaman. I guess that he reads a lot at sea. His language and grammar are so cultured. He really sounds as if he had an excellent education." She looked thoughtful. "I don't know. There is just something about him that I can't warm up to. Something that doesn't quite ring true. What does he want with us?"

"Rosa, he's lonesome," my father, the protector of lost souls, offered, "Away at sea for long periods at a time. He doesn't get a home-cooked meal for months. It's just family that he's looking for. Someplace where people speak his language. Where he can get a cup of tea. Some conversation. Home."

"I don't know. Maybe. And anyway you dream up the people you think you see."

I always found Trafeim fascinating, in small doses. He usually smelled of liquor, and his gold-toothed smile never seemed to reach his eyes. I enjoyed his harrowing stories of encounters with German submarines during Lend-Lease resupply runs to Murmansk and Vladivostok. I would watch him gesture, fascinated by his tattoo. I'd never really known anyone with a tattoo. He was an exotic addition to my provincial West Side life. Ruddy complexioned with a rolling gait and a boxer's body, he was one of Papa's charity cases. A man whose life Papa thought he could improve with one of Mama's wonderful home-made dinners and a visit to our warm and welcoming home.

"Oh. I've a letter I brought for you." Standing up, Trafeim reached into the inside pocket of his jacket and brought forth a beige parchment envelope addressed in Russian to *Abraham Sokol, Writer*, a red star was embossed on the left hand corner, under which an address was visible. "Someone brought it to me when they knew I'd see you and asked me to give it to you. I don't really know what's in it."

Papa took the letter and put it on the counter behind the table. "Thank you, I'll read it later." Mama, next to Papa at the table, looked as if she wanted to disagree.

But Papa continued, "Let's enjoy our tea. Tell me about your last voyage. And how long will you be in New York? Not the best weather."

Trafeim's visit was lengthy. I found the conversation boring. "Can I go finish my homework? I've a French test Monday."

Mama said "Study the verbs," knowing that no matter how much I studied I never got above a 70 in French, and that if I was lucky.

I could hear their voices and laughter in the kitchen until I fell asleep.

When I came in from the movies on Sunday, I had to walk around Alex and his friend Harry who were sitting in the hall flipping baseball cards. Papa and Mama were in the living room listening to WQXR.

"Turn that down a little and sit down," Mama said. She was on the low couch, her legs tucked under her, and Papa, with a book open on his lap and a cigarette in his hand, was in his favorite chair next to the window.

"*Leda*," Papa cleared his throat, "that letter that Trafeim brought. It was a government letter. From the Soviet Society of Writers and Artists. You saw that when Trafeim gave me that envelope, I put it away. I just didn't want to read it then, with him there."

Papa caught Mama's expression. "Rosa, you're not always right, not always. You don't have to keep saying you never trusted him. Heard you already. But yes. It was strange he'd have such a formal envelope to give to me. How did he even get it?" Papa passed his hand through his hair. He looked at me, and I heard pride in his voice. "The letter, the invitation, says it is honoring me, an author, with an invitation to return to the Soviet Union. It even mentions *Lubvi, Whirl of Love*, the play I wrote before the war, about the freak museum."

Mama's expression gave her feelings away.

"Why did he give it to you? How did *he* get it?" I asked. Papa gave me that look and continued.

"Why they're interested in that old play, I don't know." He took another cigarette, lit it, and recrossed his legs. "I guess they were looking through copyrights. Or library shelves. Or reviews in the Russian papers. Who knows?

"OK," Mama said. "So? What do they mean by return? You left before there even was a Soviet Union!"

"Still," Papa shrugged. "It's flattering to be remembered. The letter mentioned my work and ..." Papa pulled the letter out of his jacket pocket. "It says that 'in the interest of Soviet culture, Stalin is inviting émigré writers and artists who were born in Russia to return home.' And the letter goes on, quote 'to be contributors to the intellectual life of Mother Russia.'"

Mama did not even look at him when he was explaining this. She was paying attention to the window across the street where the tailor lived.

"What!" I turned to Papa. "To move there? To live? No! You're kidding! I'm not going anywhere. Why would you want to do that? Why would anybody?" My voice got louder and louder, afraid that my clamshell world would be disrupted by a bizarre adventure into the land of the unknown. "You're not going? Are you? You can't!"

"No. Stop! Don't get excited *Lyduce*. No. I'm just telling you what the letter that Trafeim brought said. It is flattering to be wanted as part of cultural mission—to be considered worthy of such an invitation. But no. Even though the invitation is only for me to go and see if I want to move my family there, still I won't travel so far from you and Alex and Mama. No. I'm not going."

Several months later, Mama and I were in the kitchen when Papa came home from a meeting of the Proletariat Writers and Artists Society.

"Rosa, Alexandra Tolstoy told me that she knows other people who also got invitations to move to the USSR. Funny though, none of them are Jewish." Papa's talking about this again worried me. "So I wonder why me? Why did I get that invitation and, more importantly, how did Trafeim get the letter to bring to me? A merchant marine? Just a sailor? Not government? You know, I think I have to stop seeing him. Somehow we need to distance ourselves."

"Papa ... " I started.

He interrupted me. "Shush, I'm talking to your mother. You know the whole thing stinks." He sighed. "Golovin is going. He's made up his mind."

"Golovin?" Mama echoed.

"Golovin says his letter offered amnesty if he returns to *what they call the Motherland* to help with post-war restructuring. He's packed, and he leaves next month. He's so excited. All he talks about is the boat he's going on. He's in love with it! A Soviet luxury liner." Papa smiled. "Nothing he could afford. Alexandra says whole families are packing."

Papa looked at my face. "*Lyduce*, don't worry. I'm not even thinking about it, but still I understand. The economy here stinks, and now that the soldiers are back, there are no jobs here. These old Bolsheviks like the thought of being supported. They think that their so-called Motherland will pay them to sit around and write and paint. But to take you, born in the USA, to live overseas in what kind of conditions? I don't know ... I just can't do that."

"And otherwise you'd go? You who so love New York City. Who knows every street and every alley. Over there looks so dreary and ugly and sad. In all the movies everything in Europe looks ugly and terrible," I said. "What jerks. To go there to that."

But now that I knew that Papa wasn't thinking about it, I was relieved.

"The hell with them all," Mama said. "Nothing to eat. Rubble on the streets. And Russian soldiers. God save me from Russian soldiers. If those *alter kakers* think they'll have an easy life there, they're wrong. We can't even contact the relatives the Red Cross found. The letters never get through. That's their wonderful motherland. Barbaric." Mama was getting red. "And your friend Trafeim? He's here. He called this morning. Are you planning to invite him for dinner again? He was so very interested talking to me and asked how you're doing. He went on and on about his voyage, the cargo they were carrying. I

had a hard time even getting off the phone. I told him I had to pick
up Lydia at school."

"I know he's here. He'll come for tea this evening," Papa said.

"Oh!" Mama said. I could see that her blood pressure was rising.

I came home that evening and met Trafeim and Papa in the hall
near the front door. He was just leaving, Trafeim said.

Papa looked sad when he came back into the kitchen after shut-
ting the door. Mama and I were sitting at the table.

"That was hard," Papa said. "Hard. He's a good man."

"Sure," Mama said. "Sure. Good! A good man. Yes."

"I told him that I don't think it is a good idea for us to see him
anymore. I told him that the climate in this country doesn't want
Russians to be friends with Americans, no matter what. I thought
that was the easiest way to say 'no more'. It was hard telling him
that to his face, but who the hell knows what he's up to. How did he
get that letter anyway? Why me?"

Golovin, the poet, like others who had made the choice to return
to the country of their birth, looking forward to lives of creativity
with promised honors dangled before them, disappeared into the
USSR, never to be heard from again. Years later, word reached us
that Stalin had killed most who'd returned. Those not killed went
on to live lives of deprivation and poverty in shared apartments,
scrounging for adequate food for their families.

We never heard from Trafeim again. He remains a mysterious
flicker in my life.

325 WEST 93RD STREET

Mr. Spingarn was an optician, and Mrs. Spingarn was fat and loud. She carried, below her waist, a shelf-like protuberance that undulated when she walked, a precursor of now common obese populations. She was the children's stepmother, I think.

From our fifth floor kitchen window my family peered down across the courtyard into their fourth-floor apartment. The courtyard itself was home to our Halloween adventures. It was as far as our mothers would let us go to beg for treats. We'd stand there, singing off-tune, all the children from the building, while a deluge of candy rained down on us from 24 kitchen windows above.

Life in the Spingarn household was frenetic and fun to observe. That kitchen window was our soap opera long before we acquired a television set. Every time we stood at the stove or the sink, just a glance away we could observe the ongoing drama of their household. Henrietta, their daughter, was my friend. I'd watch her pack her lunch and know that it was time to head out the door, so we could walk to school together.

There were three other children. Joey, Henrietta's little brother, played with my brother Alex. An older sister, Joan, a pretty secretary, had no love for the woman chosen by Mr. Spingarn to help raise his brood. And Richard, off in Korea, was unfortunate enough to have been drafted, or perhaps he had enlisted to avoid that tumultuous household. He was sweet, handsome in his uniform, and probably my first serious crush. The junior high school boys were all shorter than I and never smiled at me in the same indulgent way as Richie. Mr. Spingarn was a distant presence, removing himself, I always thought from the commotion he had created with this jury-rigged family.

In summer, we could hear the Spingarn family arguing in voices that echoed off the courtyard walls.

"Not cultured," my mother said.

Our apartment building was a neighborhood in itself. From the street, it looked like every other building on our side of the block. Red brick, an entrance with a blue canopy, fire escapes on which plants summered, three steps leading to a stoop that could accommodate the chairs brought down on summer evenings, where our neighbors enjoyed the breeze from the river. The lobby had marble columns and a red velvet couch. Our elevator gate and shiny brass controls were operated by Henry, an educated, well-spoken man from one of the Caribbean islands. He would shepherd us up and down while discussing American politics.

"No way I'm gonna take out citizenship in this American country. No Ma'am. I'm English and I'm proud of it. At least there I'm a person who's respected. Not like here." He'd laugh, his deep basso voice continuing, "Here, can you imagine it, I'm only three-fifths. Look at me. Do I look like three-fifths of anything? I tell you."

Our building teemed with community life. The Byrons, on the first floor, didn't pay rent because Mr. Byron was the superintendent. I had trouble understanding Mr. Byron. He spoke a funny kind of English. The family was from Alabama, white southerners who loved Henry, the black elevator man.

And there were the Zimmermans—Mrs., who wore housedresses on the street, and Mr., who always smelled of fish. Getting in the elevator with him took courage. When they moved out to the fancy new apartment building that had just been completed on Riverside Drive, my mother remarked, "Maybe the fish business wasn't so smelly after all."

There was Peter Mathews, my brother Alex's friend, whose father was always outside the building polishing his large Cadillac limousine.

My closest friends were Marty and Fred Abrahams, who lived on the fourth floor, right next to the Spingarns. Refugees from Vienna, their home had massive furniture and formal upholstery, far different from the Indian print spreads I grew up with. All of the children in the building were always respectful of Mrs. Abrahams, an elegant woman whom we nonetheless mimicked.

"Where are you going today, Mrs. Abrahams?" we would ask.

"I'm going *chopping*," she'd answer in her heavy German accent.

Actually, most of the building's tenants had accents. German, Viennese, Hungarian. They were people who were lucky enough to get out before Hitler's final curtain dropped.

On that particular Yom Kippur morning, my mother was standing by the stove making sour cream pancakes for my lunch. Although we celebrated all Jewish holidays, we did it our own way, the non-religious way. The night before, we had had our usual large family dinner. Friends of the family and relatives had arrived bearing cakes and cookies. The long table in the dining room was set with a white cloth and our blue company china. There was music and laughter and a toast to "Next year in Jerusalem," a family tradition. We sat around the table eating, laughing and talking late into the night.

Always the food was plentiful and the conversation stimulating. Papa explained to anyone who asked that we observed Jewish holidays because that "was the way our people celebrated for thousands of years." He was proud to add that he was a *Cohen*, in the line of high priests that descended directly from Aaron. Although my father preached atheism, my mother kept her own counsel. She always walked to the local synagogue on this holiday to say Yizkor, the remembrance prayer, for her parents.

But on the morning after the holiday dinner, I was tucked into my usual spot between the kitchen table and the stove. From across the courtyard, through our open windows, we could hear Mrs. Spingarn yelling.

"Put that away right now. Or I'll do it for you. What are you anyway? Some sort of a *goy*, a gentile? Don't you know how to listen? What's wrong with you? Every year the same thing. How come you just never remember that this is a holy day? What's wrong with you?"

"Get the hell away from me," I heard Joan say. I got up to look. Mama turned from the stove, and now the two of us were positioned together with a clear view of the drama unfolding across the courtyard. Joan was standing at the ironing board. "Who the hell are you anyway to tell me what to do, you dumb bitch! Get away from me. Go do something else if you don't like it," she yelled.

"You put that iron and ironing board away. Right now! Not in my kitchen. It's not the time for that. On Yom Kippur. What are you anyway? You live here free. Get out if you don't like it. If you can't live right, go live where there are people like you." We could see her push Joan's shoulder.

"You dumb bitch," Joan's voice started to crack. "Get away from me, or I'll make you get away." She put the iron face down on the board and headed across the kitchen to the silverware drawer.

Before I even knew what Mama was doing, she turned off the flame under the frying pan and ran down the long hall to the door. Within what seemed like a second, I saw Joan with a knife in her hand and my mother restraining her. And then I watched my mother take the knife away and put her arm around Joan, leading her, weeping, past Mrs. Spingarn. Out of my sight. Out of their kitchen. I saw Mrs. Spingarn sit down heavily at their table and put her head on her arms, her body shaking.

And then Joan was in our kitchen. Mama turned on the flame again and flipped the pancakes. Then she walked into the other room to set up the ironing board so Joan could iron the blouse she planned to wear to synagogue.

Joan sat at our table crying. My mother, in her usual role of counselor, sat down next to her, explaining that she could either listen to Mrs. Spingarn's rules or move out.

Apartment house dramas unfolded constantly, but the best were those we saw from the kitchen window. And the members of the Spingarn family were often the *dramatis personae*.

One evening, I was walking home from a friend's house. She lived on Central Park West. Papa always asked that I call before I set out to come home, and he would then wait for me on the stoop, stewarding me with his line-of-sight view down 93rd Street. As I approached, he walked down the steps to meet me.

"*Lyduce*." He looked sad. "I've something to tell you." He put his arm around my shoulders and hugged me to him. "Richie was killed." He stopped, allowing me to have a reaction.

I looked at him in disbelief. "Killed? Richie? Oh my God." I looked at Papa's face, hoping that somehow I'd misunderstood.

"His body is going to be shipped back home."

This was before teenaged Suzy Dunn, an upstairs neighbor, took her own life. At the time, I still believed that only old people died.

Richie. My Richie, I thought. A deep pain in my heart. I don't remember what I said. But I do remember that Papa, always philosophical about life and death, hugged me to him, letting me absorb the horror. Together we stood there feeling the wind off the river and the chill of the winter to come.

"Life goes on, *Lyduce*. Life goes on. You will get up tomorrow morning and go to school. And your friends will be there. And your teachers. Life goes on. I don't know how to explain. I just don't know."

The Spingarn family continued to live in that fourth floor apartment. Joan eventually got married to a good-looking young sailor. My friend Henrietta went out with a tall, athletic blond boy who lived on 94th Street. Joey and my brother Alex and their friend Peter remain in touch. But the Spingarn household was never again as noisy or boisterous or frenetic as it had been.

But, as Papa said, life went on.

LAMBCHOPS

I had just gotten off the Black and Tan Line camp bus that was still standing on 17th Street, in front of the building where a variety of left-wing organizations were headquartered. I turned 15 that June, and this was my second summer at Camp Wo-Chi-Ca.

I enjoyed the grand sense of independence that was available to me at camp, where I could be alone, make my own decisions, and meet different kinds of people. There we sang of a world that was ours for the making. A world where people of all races could live together in friendship, where children of the working class could be leaders in the struggle for a new world order.

Mama and Papa belonged to the IWO, The International Workers Order, and through that organization they had cemetery insurance, a health plan with doctors that charged a five-dollar co-payment, and the opportunity to send their children away for the summer—to Wo-Chi-Ca, *Worker's Children's Camp,* in Port Murray, New Jersey. From today's vantage point, I see that ideas once considered radical have become commonplace in the thinking of the nation.

Later, during the McCarthy years, such entitlements were considered socialist at best, and the IWO was put on the Attorney General's Watch List. The benefits were disbanded, and the cemetery insurance was taken over by the government and distributed to private firms. Mama and Papa were left with the fear of being accused of being Communist sympathizers based on their IWO membership.

Papa had been waiting with the other parents when the bus pulled up. His smile stiffened when he saw that I was sitting with a boy's arm on the back of my seat. As I got to him, pulling the boy along, he gave me a big hug and took my bag from me.

"Papa, this is Lambchops," I said, introducing my summer boyfriend—actually, my boyfriend for only the last week.

"Hello," Papa said. "Hello," he hesitated and then said, "Lambchops."

"Let's go," said Papa. "Say your goodbyes and let's go." With Papa waiting anxiously, I hugged a few camp mates and said a hasty goodbye to a startled Lambchops. Papa took my elbow and propelled me towards the subway.

"Yes. I'll put you on the bus to Pinewood tomorrow morning." Papa said as if continuing a conversation he was having with himself. "Yes, tomorrow you go."

"Papa, I'm supposed to stay in the city with you until Mama and Alex come home from the country next Saturday." I wasn't supposed to join them in Pinewood. That was never the plan, for me to go to the country. I'd been there too many years already.

He was hurrying me along. "Lambchops. What kind of a name is that?"

"No, Papa, that's not his real name. It's a nickname."

"Strange name," Papa said.

"Not for camp, Papa."

We all had nicknames that summer. There was Benji from New Jersey and Whitey with the blond hair. I still wonder if Crisco (as in *fat in the can*) really liked her name. And there was curly-haired Jerry, who went on to become Jerry Silverman the folk singer, who was older and had all the girls' hearts humming.

That summer was a special one at camp. The boys and some parents who volunteered their time finally completed the recreation and drama building that had been in progress for two summers. "Gotta get it built in time for visiting weekend and the dedication," was the mantra of the summer. Nobby, who was a senior camper, was in charge of the work detail, and I would watch in awe as he instructed the certified volunteer adults in carpentry and cement laying. Each weekend new groups of fathers would arrive on the bus from New York, in their suits and ties and hats. They spent the weekend in the director's house and emerged in a variety of work outfits ready to help tackle the installation of this new structure.

The new building was shiny and rounded, a surplus U.S. Army Quonset hut that had been purchased with money raised through donations from the parents and the Organization. It was set on a cement slab, and a large concrete amphitheater was constructed outside the hanger door. That way a performance could be seen from both inside or outside, depending on the weather. The shiny metal building remains beautiful in my memory.

We named it The Paul Robeson Playhouses. Paul Robeson was by then known not only as an All-American professional athlete and a Phi Beta Kappa laureate but also for his wonderful bass-baritone singing voice and as the first black actor to achieve long running fame as Othello on Broadway. He was a trade unionist and a forerunner of the civil rights movement, and although he had received worldwide fame for artistic achievement, his union and liberal activism would soon bring him to the attention of Senator Joseph McCarthy.

In my camp yearbook, there is a picture of our dedication ceremony. There is Paul Robeson wearing a flowered shirt sitting with five young campers. Next to him, dwarfed by his size, are a tow-haired boy in a striped polo and several little girls dressed in skirts and blouses with saddle shoes and white socks. One girl wearing penny loafers is looking with wonder at the tall smiling man. In another picture I am sitting on the floor together with a large group of campers. We have song sheets in our hands and are solemnly watching something in front of us, now unseen and forgotten.

By end of the following summer, local farmers had equated integration with communism and made life unsafe for campers and staff. The camp was closed, and Robeson's concert in Peekskill, NY, had provoked a riot of such proportion that it tore through the town, through Westchester County and as far down as Harlem, while police stood idly by doing nothing. But that summer I, ever apolitical and in fact bored at the Saturday morning camp lectures on world order, looked at the coming of Robeson as an event that would allow us, the campers, to see a world figure, a singer of international stature who would come to our camp to visit. And to perform for us, the children of Camp Wo-Chi-Ca.

Other international figures visited our camp as well. I remember a man whose name I think was Liu Lang-Mo, ostensibly a figure in the Chinese workers revolution, being introduced in our dining hall. He was quite small, very unimpressive, but treated with great respect. He spoke to us in rather good English about political matters that most of us campers cared little about. "Small man," said Nobby. "He sure couldn't swing a hammer for the people."

Union leaders too would arrive periodically. They were self-important men who expected the director and staff to parade them around. The campers usually saw them in the dining hall where they would be introduced and feted. So and so from the ILGWU. Or another from the AFL. We would clap respectfully and then continue with our lunch and singing.

Our songs each summer were workers' songs, union songs, songs about freedom and equality. Some were classic such as "Goodnight, Irene," "On Top of Old Smokey," "Tzena, Tzena Tzena." These, although non-political, were still culturally identified with "the people." Others were indeed political: "John Henry," "Working On the Railroad," songs about the Jews' fight for Palestine, the Negroes' fight for equal rights, and songs about a China freed from Chiang Kai-Shek. And our favorite: "If I had a hammer, I'd hammer for freedom; I'd hammer for justice, all over this land." We worshiped Walt Whitman. We loved Woody Guthrie and Pete Seeger. And we sang and sang and sang. Our camp was not only about sports and spirit. Our camp, we were told and believed, was about making a better world, a world where swords would be beaten into plowshares, where justice would prevail and where all people would live as brothers.

And now I had to go to the country and live with chickens, cows, the large bull in the field, and *Babushka*, the woman who presided over that rural kingdom. Before he went to work the following morning, Papa took me to the Trailways Bus Station. We sat in the waiting room until they called the Pinewood bus and then descended into the fume-filled bus terminal. I had my small red suitcase that I'd hastily packed the night before, foraging in my camp trunk overstuffed with dirty laundry for a bathing suit, some polo shirts, sweaters and pants. Remembering *Babushka's* iron-clad rules about neat clothes for Sunday dinner, I also packed a short tan skirt and a lacy blouse. Papa kissed me good-bye and helped me up the steps. I found a seat behind the driver and unhappily waited for the beginning of my trip.

Sitting on the bus, through the tunnel and down the Jersey Turnpike, I kept reviewing the events of the previous day, trying to figure out why Papa had made me go to Pinewood even through the original plan was to stay on 93rd Street. I thought about what Papa could have seen through the bus window that disturbed him. A bus full of tired and happy campers pulling to a stop while parents waited on the sidewalk. Lambchops and me together sitting on the side of the bus nearest the curb. But that couldn't be it, I thought. Certainly Papa knew that boys were part of my life. I hung around on Broadway and in the Riverside Drive playgrounds with boys. Some came to our house as well, and both Papa and Mama were cordial and welcoming. And Lambchops did not even have his hand on my shoulder. Thinking about it later, I wondered if perhaps it was his tawny skin.

ROOMERS

Roomers were a staple of my growing up. Not boarders, because boarders would have had what Mama called *kitchen privileges*. Roomers did not violate our family space. That was, unless Mama befriended them, in which case they would sit at the kitchen table, drinking tea and telling Mama their woes. Mama read Freud, loved Isadora Duncan and Margaret Sanger, strong women both, and believed in a woman's right to choose before that term was coined. Her counseling skills and her level headed advice, so useful to her roomers, served her well when, at age 58, she started working for New York State Employment.

After all of these years, I can only remember the names of a few. The rest remain unidentified and unimportant. Mr. Yamaguchi, who roomed with us when we still lived on 136th Street in an apartment where the rooms were off a large foyer, was a slim, polite, and elegant young man. His black hair was shiny, and although he was not very tall, he carried himself with almost military starch. He wore suits and ties and often a black felt fedora. He worked for a firm that was located somewhere in the financial district.

I have pictures of him standing against a stone wall on Riverside Drive, smiling at the camera. In one, his hand rests on my shoulder, and my cousin Bess, older than me by fifteen years and thus closer to his age, is on my other side. From the picture, I deduce that we had gone for a walk on a nice spring day, and someone, probably Papa, had snapped the picture to commemorate our pleasures. Mr. Yamaguchi disappeared from my life one day. I must have been at school, because I don't remember his leaving. Nor did it dawn on me for many years that his disappearance was linked to political necessity. I think he left our home not long before the day that Japanese planes attacked Pearl Harbor. I've often wondered if he really wanted to leave or if he was called back. Papa and Mama never really spoke about him after that. I suspect that they were frightened that his living with us would bring trouble to our family.

Our apartment on 93rd Street was L-shaped. Every time we came or went, we had to pass the two rooms where the roomers lived. But the front of the apartment with its wide windows, large rooms and a view of the Hudson, was our private quarters. I had a bathroom of my own because I lived in what was once "the maid's room," but the rest of the family shared with these other people. I came and went, I now realize, ignoring these roomers' existence, their foreignness, their loneliness and the fact that they were indeed part of my mother's life. My parents, I now realize, never really could ignore them. Although my father always bragged, "My wife does not have to work," she cleaned their rooms weekly and provided them with fresh towels and sheets. When the Chinese laundry man delivered these, she carefully noted in his presence the count of those she sent out, gave him a copy and put the other under the hall telephone.

Our rent was covered by these roomers. They were often students, single people new to the city, in need of housing and in need of mothering, too. And mothering many of them got. Some, businessmen or -women who left early and worked late, just came and went. But for the others, the young, the Columbia University students or the ones from NYU, Mama was always available to give advice, to counsel, to suggest and if the roomer was a young woman, to insist on proper social behavior. Ours was not a house to which these roomers could bring company without permission. And permission was given, if at all, after careful vetting and long conversations.

Mr. Hiff lived with us for about six months. He was different from anyone I had ever met. He came from Wichita, Kansas. How strange that mention of that city still brings to mind a man so far in my past. I think I must have had a childhood crush on him—his differentness, his movie star qualities—his American-ness and Midwest politeness to me and to my parents. He'd stand at the door to the kitchen talking about the weather and the latest news. His suits were well-tailored, and the cuffs of his shirts had his initials on them. Sometimes he wore a V-necked sweater under his jacket, giving him a very Henry Fonda look. Mama once commented that he was depressed, a Freudian analysis that she proceeded to explain to me. She said she understood why he had left home to work in a new place, one that held no memories for him. But he too disappeared one day. I probably did not even notice that for at least a week, since our encounters were so infrequent.

And then there was Heddi. She was probably in her late thirties when she moved in. She lived with us for many years and later moved into the apartment building next door to ours. She became a fixture in our lives. In an apartment building where neighbors became friends, Heddi became one of the locals. She knew the Spingarns who lived on the fourth floor and became good friends with their daughter Joan. She picked up groceries for Mrs. Dunn if she happened to be going up to Broadway. And on hot summer evenings before the air conditioner changed neighborhood social contacts, she joined other neighbors who often did not go back upstairs until late at night after the heat subsided. I remember having to pass through this crowd returning from my evening tours of Broadway. That group of neighbors sitting on the front steps were the sentries of the neighborhood. They knew who came and went, and they carefully reported which teenagers came home late and which were inappropriately dressed. "Did you have a good time tonight, Lydia?" one of them always asked.

Mother took Heddi on as another family member. I was almost a teenager by then and would come home from school to find Mama and Heddi sitting at the kitchen table enjoying a cup of tea and a pastry. I know that Heddi worked as a bookkeeper, yet in my memory she was always at that table. And I was gratified that I could pass through to my room without having to deal with my mother's questions about school, friends or grades. I think, looking back, that I was glad that these roomers took up my mother's curiosity, thus allowing me my own space and Americanized world. I think.

Heddi was round and short with an infectious laugh. Black hair in large round curlers, she would sit with my mother drinking tea and gossiping about the other people in her life, her job, and her favorite topic—the New York Yankees. The New York Yankees were her surrogate family. She had crushes on most of the players and adored or hated Casey Stengel depending on the season. Alex and I benefited from her passion. We would often accompany her to Yankee games, and because of her personalization of the team, we felt that Mickey Mantle, Phil Rizzuto and Whitey Ford were family. We would bring home our scorecards, walks and runs accurately penciled in. We became baseball fanatics. At night, lying in bed, I'd listen to Heddi's team, believing that if I thought hard enough, if I said "strike him out, strike him out" enough times, I would be able to send that message through the air and determine the route of the ball toward the batter and the direction of the swing.

One night I was trying to make arrangements to meet my friend Rosalie on the corner. On warm evenings Broadway became the parade ground of teenage Westsiders. Our route, from 96th Street (no one *ever* went above 96th) to 72nd, was our social world. Each landmark, Teresa's Drug Store on 81st and the Optimo Cigar store on 79th, was the meeting ground of particular groups of teenagers. I still remember the membership of these cliques, which temple their families belonged to, and their reputations as spoiled rich kids or stickball advocates. Knowing who you were to meet and what time to gather was of prime importance to teenaged life.

Our telephone sat on a short bookcase in the long hall right before the turn into the front part of our apartment. In those days phones were not the ubiquitous necessity that they've become, and our roomers were not encouraged to make calls. But if they had to, they were required to leave change in the flowered bowl near the telephone. Mama insisted that all calls be short. But for Heddi it was different. She talked and talked, laughing and gossiping with her girlfriends long into the night.

Calling Rosalie was very important to me. I believed deep down in my teenage heart that my whole social life depended on knowing what our evening plans were. But Heddi kept on talking and talking. Several times I walked over to where she was sitting, squished on a small stool next to the telephone books, talking away, and whispered to her, "I have to make a call." Each time she ignored me.

"Get off the phone please," I whispered, to no response, and went back to the kitchen to wait for her to hang up. I sat at the table for a few minutes and then returned to the hall. Heddi was still talking, and not only that, but she didn't even look at me.

"Get off the phone, Heddi," I hissed. I stood next to her with my hand on my hip obviously listening to her conversation and making faces.

"Heddi, get off the phone! I have to call Ros now! Hang up." She continued talking. I returned to the kitchen, incensed that she was ignoring me. *Me,* a member of the family!

I stomped toward her, hands on hips, footsteps audible. "This is not your home. Get off the phone!" I yelled. I was irate. A wronged teenager demanding my rights.

Then I did it. I put my finger on the cradle of the phone and hung it up for her. "This is NOT your home," I yelled.

Heddi stormed into the kitchen to tell my mother. I called Rosalie and proudly told her what I'd done, and then we talked about where we would meet and whom we'd see on Broadway that evening.

Mama was very angry with me. "How can you do that? It was so rude!" she lectured, Heddi standing behind me at the kitchen door. "Apologize to Heddi. It's not polite to treat a grown-up that way."

I sullenly mumbled an "I'm sorry" and slammed into my room. I checked my hair in the mirror over my desk, made sure that my loafers were shiny and that I had money in my purse, and walked past them to the door. I was off to Broadway.

Heddi didn't talk to me for weeks, but I certainly didn't care. She was a stranger in *my* house, and although my mother was her friend, it was my house, my home and she was, for me, just another in a stream of unimportant residents.

I'm not sure how soon after that Heddi moved into the next building. But when spring came we continued our Yankee game excursions, at least for a while.

By the time I was in college, the roomers had become a different breed. Mr. Houser had moved in by then. He was a lonesome little man, a refugee. He lived in the room right next to the door, not working, being supported by a brother in South America. He was taciturn and unrevealing, but I understood that he had survived life in a concentration camp.

And the large room next to Mr. Hauser's became home to a variety of my college friends, strays that I would bring home so that they could avail themselves of my mother's sensible advice. I was quite content to donate them to her while I kept my own counsel and solved my own social dilemmas. By then I was happy to be released from my mother's care, and I was happy to give her lost souls to mother.

THE LIST

When Carol, Dr. Shapiro's wife and receptionist, answered the door, she said, "Oh, Lydia. Hello." She kept her hand on the door. "Is the Doctor expecting you?"

Strange, I thought. Not her usual friendly greeting.

"No," I said, "Uh ... uh. Is it all right?"

I had just come from Joan of Arc, the Junior High School next door to the doctor's office. I often dropped in at odd hours just to talk. His five-dollar fee, part of my parents' International Worker's Organization insurance plan, was certainly reasonable for the care our family got. I thought of him as an uncle, one whose door was always open to me.

"Well ... " She motioned for me to come inside. I followed her into the large reception room with its Oriental rug and heavy leather furniture. Tall plants on the two wide windowsills blocked a view of the sidewalk.

"Doctor is not too happy today." Carol was the doctor's barometer, but the mood was usually sunny in their world.

Today she walked heavily, her chunky heels clicking on the wooden floor. She turned to me. "He was in the hospital doing rounds this morning, but when he came in ... Oh, well." she shrugged, "He always enjoys your company. Go right in."   She opened the door to his office. "Philip, dear. Lydia's here."

Dr. Shapiro was sitting at his desk, his chin in his hand.

He looked up. "Lydia. Do come on in." He sat up straighter. "Come in, and sit yourself down."

"Doctor, my mother said I should stop by so you could check my knee. She said she didn't like the way it looked."

I sat down on the edge of the maroon leather chair that stood in front of his desk. As usual, I tried to keep my eyes away from the man-sized skeleton that stood in the corner between a tall cabinet and a wall of bookcases lined with thick medical texts.

Balding, overweight and looking like a movie priest, he was the closest thing to a father confessor that I had. Not only did he cure my earaches and sore throats, but also he resolved girlfriend problems and parental disputes, dispensing calming benedictions and sage advice. My brother Alex also loved to visit. When he came with Mama, he always brought the new *aggie* and *immie* marbles that he'd added to his collection. Alex told me that sometimes Dr. Shapiro actually got down on the floor and shot a few with him. Mama said he really did, but I just couldn't imagine *that*.

But today, the Doctor seemed different, distracted. He put his chin back on his hand. "Yes, dear?" he said.

"Well," I hesitated. "Dr. Shapiro, do you think this is getting infected?" I lifted my pleated skirt to show him a crusty sore.

I also wanted to tell him that I had gotten an A on the report that I'd talked to him about. It was about puerperal fever, the infection that had killed my grandmother after she'd given birth to my mother. I'd spent my whole last visit asking him questions, and he had helped me to organize my thoughts.

"Dr. Shapiro," I said, "If this isn't a good time, it's OK. I'll just come back."

"No. No. It's quite OK. Why don't you just come over here?" He motioned me to his side of the desk. I was glad we weren't heading for the examining room with its paper covered table and shiny medical instruments displayed on a metal tray.

"Let me look at that knee. Ah." He stood up and walked over to the cabinet next to the skeleton. "Here." He took a tube of ointment out of a drawer. "I think if you put this on twice a day your knee will be just fine." He looked at me. "Lydia, you'll be fine. Your knee will be fine. But I'll tell you, I'm not so sure about our country. Not so sure at all." He paused. "Oh well, dear. That's not your problem. Not yet." I wasn't sure what he was talking about, so I just nodded.

When I put the five dollars that Mama had given me for him on his desk, he waved his hand. "No, not today. Not today at all."

He walked with me to the door. "Come back in a week, and let me see that knee. Go ahead now. And say hello to Rosa and Abram. I'm sure they're not so happy either today."

"But Dr. Shapiro. Why? Why wouldn't they not be happy?"

"Oh, Lydia. It's a long story. I just don't know. First the Russians are our friends, and then anyone who belongs to an organization that helped them during the war is considered dangerous. Now we're all Communists. Criminals. But Lydia, you go ahead now. Put that salve on, and you'll be fine."

I made my way down 93rd Street, favoring my knee but enjoying the breeze that came off the river. P.S. 93, my brother's school, had just let out, so I stayed on the south side of the street to avoid their rowdy class dismissal. Kids were running everywhere. When I reached Broadway, I stopped at Papaya Joe's and bought myself a frank with a part of the five dollars I still held in my hand. I added lots of mustard from the squeeze bottle on the counter.

"Mama," I said when I walked into the kitchen. "Here's change from the money that you gave me for Dr. Shapiro. He said to keep it so I bought a frank. He was really strange today." But Mama wasn't listening. She had the *PM* newspaper in front of her and was checking something.

"What?" She looked up at me. Papa, who was sitting across from her, had the *New York Post* spread out. It covered the sugar bowl that was usually at the center of our kitchen table, and part of it was on the paper Mama was looking at. I gave them both a kiss *hello* and started for my room, off of the kitchen. "How was school?" Mama asked.

"Fine, thanks."

Sitting at my desk, flush against the kitchen wall, I eavesdropped on their conversation. They were speaking Yiddish so I knew that their conversation was secret, not for my ears, unlike the Russian we all spoke at home and the English we used elsewhere. But I understood more Yiddish than they knew, learned from prior eavesdropping occasions. They were talking about a list, *The Attorney General's List,* in the papers in front of them. I heard them say that the IWO was on the list.

Papa's voice was fearful, as usual. "I was never really so interested in the IWO politics. Rosa, you know that."

"So? Interested or not interested, it is what it is, at this point." I knew she was trying to calm Papa down.

But Papa continued. "Those bastards forget about us working people. The IWO was our way to have a doctor and a cemetery plot. Even a camp for Lydia to go to." I could hear the rustling of the newspaper. "Now we're all Communists." His voice got louder. "It's not Communist to have medical insurance. And what happens with the cemetery policy? I've paid into it for years." Their voices got lower, and although I couldn't hear what they were saying, I understood that the *list* they were talking about would somehow change their lives.

I walked back into the kitchen. I forgot that I wasn't supposed to understand Yiddish.

"Mama. Do you think that is why Dr. Shapiro was so upset? That *list*? I told you. He was different."

"Of course. Everyone's upset. I'm upset. Papa's upset."

Papa, I knew, lived upset. He always had a mental suitcase packed, afraid that he'd have to run from another place, as he had from Russia. A Jew and a foreigner, an intellectual. And now, part of an organization that the Attorney General, *the United States* Attorney General, considered threatening and subversive. I had trouble understanding Papa's fears. This was America, after all. *My* country. A fair country. Why would Dr. Shapiro be upset about the *list,* I wondered. After all he was born here. He wasn't an immigrant like Papa and Mama.

Mama closed the paper. "I'll make dinner. Lydia, go do your homework. We won't eat for a while."

I soon forgot about Papa's fears and Mama's worries. My life consisted of Broadway strolls, movies, flirting, and school. I'd read the paper once in a while but not the political articles. I was more interested in human-interest stories and Hollywood gossip.

I was in high school when the IWO was finally disbanded. But the June following my visit to the doctor, Mama and I were in the kitchen waiting for Papa to come home. We heard the door open and then footsteps coming down the hall. Papa walked in still wearing his coat and hat. He dropped his folded newspaper on the table and fumbled with his top coat button.

"Rosa." He put his hat on the table, something he never did. "I ran into Mrs. Shapiro on Broadway. I stopped to say hello She was all in black. I knew the minute I saw her that someone had died."

"Who?" Mama picked up Papa's hat. "Abram. Who died?"

"Philip. The doctor." Papa sat down heavily. "Dr. Shapiro. He died."

"No?" Mama said. "No? Philip?"

Papa nodded. "I said 'what happened?' And she said, Rosa, it was so strange how she said it. She said, 'he's gone. He wanted to go and so he did.' And then she kind of patted my shoulder and started walking away. 'Take care of your beautiful family,' she said."

I never knew the whole story. I don't know if my parents did either. But for a long time after that we went to a New York City Health Center for our medical care.

THE COUSINS

Aunt Fanny opened the door.

"Rosa, Abram. Welcome, welcome. Come in. Lydia, don't you look nice in your velvet coat? And Alex, look at you." She patted his blond hair. "What a big boy you are. Almost five, no? Look at that. It doesn't even look like hair. It looks like a gold halo on your head."

Alex, standing there holding Papa's hand, looked confused but smiled anyway.

"Go ahead in, Rosa, Abram." Fanny put her hand on my mother's shoulder. "That little boy is a real gift." My mother smiled.

Tall, imperial, with a pince-nez hanging from her neck and her grey hair arranged around her head in a crown, Fanny was the picture of self-assurance. She smiled at the elevator man, who was still standing in front of the mirrored cage in which we had arrived.

Fanny stood back to let us in. I'd been in Fanny and Mirosha's apartment many times, but now I saw it anew. On the round table in the middle of the foyer, reaching almost to the bottom of the crystal chandelier, was a tall vase full of red and pink lilies. Echoing them across the room, atop the grand piano, were more flowers. Elegantly dressed grown-ups were standing in small groups smiling, gesturing and patting each other's shoulders, women kissing cheeks, men laughing loudly. What an anniversary party, I thought.

"Give Mimi your coats and find Mirosha. Natalie is right over there with her medical school friends."

Mimi, Fanny's housekeeper and friend, had lived with my aunt and her family for many years. She cooked, cleaned, answered the door and generally made sure that life in Fanny and Mirosha's household ran smoothly.

"Yes. Please welcome. May I have your coats," Mimi said. With her French accent it sounded like *your cats*. "Please. Please go ahead in."

My uncle Mirosha and his wife Fanny, my mother's first cousin, were both doctors at Mount Sinai Hospital. He was a surgeon, and Fanny was an obstetrician-gynecologist. I knew that she was my mother's doctor for womanly things. Fanny's brother Geoffrey and sister Betty were doctors as well. Papa and Mama loved the fact that their relatives whose lives had started in Kishinov were able to enter major medical careers here in America.

"You should go to medical school," they'd tell me, ignoring my less than exemplary grades in science.

Mirosha's booming voice cut through the crowd. "Rose. Abram. Hello. *Lydushka*, come be introduced." Cigarette in hand, gray hair pomaded, he waved us on. He was standing with a group of men, all of whom smiled as we approached. They broadened their circle to enclose us. Their white cuffs shone against the black of their tuxedos.

"These are Fanny's cousins, Rose and Abram Sokolovsky. And this is their daughter Lydia and little *Shurik*. Beautiful children, no?" Mirosha declaimed.

"This is Stephen Bailick." Mirosha pounded the man next to him on the shoulder. "He and I operate together every Wednesday. And I've known him and his family ever since I got to America. I call him *my Yankee* because he was born in Brooklyn and went to medical school here. Not like me." His laugh was infectious. It came from deep in his ample belly and made the gold chain attached to the middle button of his vest and trailing down into his pants pocket move up and down. It had several gold keys attached to it, and I knew that at the end was a gold watch. "And these fellows are the rest of the important medical staff. Ha, ha!"

Mirosha guided us past the entrance to the library, where a group of men gathered around the new Magnavox TV.

We barely had time to say hello before we were urged on. "Betty and Misha are over there. They are holding court. Come with me," Mirosha said in his booming voice, laughing. "Family, family. It's nice to have family. Ha. Ha." He took Alex's hand and made his way through the tightly packed room. "Marsha, hello. Bernie, how are you? Steven, how is your little daughter?" He never stopped his banter as he maneuvered us along with him. Finally we reached the family.

"Rosa, Alex," Betty hugged my mother. "Lydia, Abram. How are you?"

"Good, good," my mother answered. "Misha, I walked right past your building last week. Is that Yorkville Plumbing sign new?"

"No, I had to repaint it. After all of these years it's gotten hard to read." Tall, thin, elegant Uncle Misha, a Russian engineer turned plumbing contractor, was one of my favorite family members.

"We haven't seen you all for so long." Betty took over for her husband, as she usually did. "Work. Responsibilities. Meetings. Life gets too busy. But I know that Geoffrey was at your house last week when Lydia had that ear infection. Too much swimming, huh? *Leda*, how do you feel now?"

"I'm OK now, thank you. But it really hurt before Uncle Geoffrey came." Misha and Betty's conversation with my parents continued. I stood there listening, looking around.

The room was getting more crowded, but I saw that Mother and Father were having a good time, talking, exchanging news and laughing. Alex, holding onto my mother's hand, was fidgeting. I shifted from foot to foot, trying not to look bored.

Mirosha patted me on the shoulder. "Go say hello to Natalie," he said. "She's over there. Her medical school friends love coming to our parties, but I don't see them enough the rest of the time. Studying all the time, Natalie tells us."

He turned to my parents. "That's what young people do. Study, huh? I hope they leave a little time for love. Yes. Go, go, Lydia. Speak to the young people."

I had never really spent any time with Natalie, and yet I felt that I had to move in that direction. I walked across the room.

"Hi, Natalie. How are you? " I said.

"This is my cousin Lydia," Natalie said. She smiled at me. I felt uncomfortable, knowing I had interrupted their conversation.

"It's nice to see you," she said. She paused. "How's school?"

"Fine, thank you," I smiled. "How is your school?"

Natalie said "Good." But there was now a vacuum, and, not knowing how to fill it, I started back into the crowd. I looked back longingly at those sophisticated young people. They looked so comfortable together.

I sat down on a burgundy velvet love seat next to the piano. Behind me, standing next to the wall, were three women dressed in long gowns. They were talking in quiet voices, apparently sharing secrets. Trying to look uninterested, I tuned in to their conversation. Eavesdropping was fun.

The oldest one, whose gray hair matched her silver dress and shoes, was talking in what she thought was a quiet voice.

"She's marvelous. So protective of her patients. I just love Fanny. Amazing gynecologist! So ahead of her time. And brave, too, what with the law so strict. Although I know that at Mount Sinai they try to help as best they can. That's only a rumor, of course. God forbid it's anything official, you know. Right, Diana?" She looked at the woman next to her.

"I don't know. Maybe the doctors talk among themselves, but ... "

"I hear women come here, and she does it right in her home office," the gray-haired lady interrupted. "A friend told me about it. Did you know about it, Diana?"

"Of course I knew about it. I was here when I was pregnant with Max, and I saw a girl leave Fanny's office looking so pale and uncomfortable. But you know. What else could Fanny do? Let her use a hanger and kill herself? And when I asked, Fanny told me that the girl was not even married and that the boy was a soldier on his way to Korea. A student in college. Fanny said the girl didn't even tell her parents. Fanny is so brave."

"But Diana, do you really think she should do this?" the third woman, whose name I still hadn't heard, whispered. "I certainly don't. Not if it's illegal, if for no other reason. And there are other reasons, too, as far as I'm concerned." She clutched her shawl to her and looked around to make sure no one heard her.

Diana's voice got stronger. "Of course, I think she should do it. I completely agree with Fanny. She believes that a woman's body is her own and that she has a right to choose her life."

"Shush!" The gray-haired woman said. "You don't want anyone to hear. And Natalie is standing right over there. It's against the law what Fanny is doing. We shouldn't be talking about this anyway." She glanced around her at the guests near the table.

"OK. You're right. Let's go get something to eat. The food looks wonderful." The one whose name I now knew was Diana put her arm around the gray-haired woman's waist, and they moved away.

I knew that they had no idea I'd been listening, if they had even noticed me. I was sitting there, peeling my nail polish and looking as if I was thinking about something, maybe dreaming. And anyway, I was just a teenager. Not important to them, of course.

I sat there on that sofa while the three women moved away, and then I wandered back to where my parents were standing. I made my way across the room, weaving around people holding plates and balancing glasses of champagne, all the while trying to digest the gravity of what I'd heard.

I loved visiting Fanny and Mirosha. Natalie was rarely there, and I really did not feel that I knew her at all. That their world was so different from ours was made irrelevant by the warmth and embrace of her parents. And I knew that they dispensed their medical skills freely when family was involved. Now I knew Fanny's generosity included strangers as well. I moved back to where Alex and my parents were standing, still talking to Betty and Misha.

"We don't get to see you often enough, not like Geoffrey does," Betty smiled at me. "Geoffrey does his home visits and gets to eat your Mama's wonderful *Bef Stroganoff* and winter borscht. And that rye bread your Papa brings home from Cake Masters. He teases me that Fanny sees Mama for woman's stuff but the food is better on his home visits. Misha and I, we don't see you often enough."

Betty always looked stern, but I knew that was only her look. Maybe it was those clear, frameless glasses that made her seem so serious, or her choice of tailored suits and low heeled shoes. Doctor's clothes. Her freely dispensed hugs to her ample bosom left me struggling for air.

"I'm looking forward to this New Year's Eve," she continued. "Geoffrey has tickets for the opera. You're coming, right?" My uncle Geoffrey had never married. He lived with what the family sarcastically called his secretary. When we visited she would disappear into the back of his apartment after a perfunctory hello and never reappear again. He never took her to the opera or to family parties but she was always in the background, the subject of family concern, gossip and disapproval.

I left Mama, Papa and Alex and wandered through the apartment, replaying the overheard conversation. Large dark pieces of Biedermeier furniture, imported from Vienna and polished to a reflecting sheen, were positioned against the walls. An enormous table, surrounded by guests reaching for caviar and blini, stood against the dining room wall. A tall black man was deftly manipulating plates and serving pieces, and Mimi was helping to dish out cold meat and red potato salad from a large tureen.

Going down in the elevator, on our way home, I continued replaying the overheard conversation.

"Mama," I asked in Russian. "Did you know that Aunt Fanny does abortions in her house?" I was sitting next to her on the crosstown bus. Papa and my brother were across the aisle. I wasn't sure if this was a subject that I should bring up now, but I felt that I had learned something of great importance. "Did you know that she helps women not kill themselves with hangers?"

Mama moved closer to me. "Don't talk so loudly," she whispered. "Even in Russian. We'll talk about this later."

I had just put on my pajamas when Mama came into my room. She sat down on my bed and patted it for me to join her. "Lydia, I want to explain about Aunt Fanny. About what she does. It's illegal and secret, and she could not only lose her license but also go to jail. You asked me whether I know. Of course I know. But we mustn't ever talk about it. And you can't say anything to anyone, not your friends or anybody." She put her arm around me and brought me closer. "But of course I know. I know all about it." Her face looked different. Almost as if she had a secret too.

"She is a skilled doctor, your cousin, and a good woman. I can't tell you how indebted I am to her." She sighed. "Sometimes a family just can't afford to feed another mouth and sometimes men aren't careful. Fanny is a protector of women. We are all safe in her hands." Mama looked at me and pulled me closer. "We should all be grateful that there are doctors like Fanny. A hero. Yes, a savior."

I'd never even talked about abortion to anyone. My friends and I, still in Junior High School, had just read *Forever Amber*. We'd reread the few sex scenes in the book to each other, giggling at innuendos we hardly understood. Now I had something new to bring them: abortion. Something exciting to share.

Years passed before I met Natalie again. I was married and had children of my own when, one day, Mama called me to say that Natalie had gotten in touch with her.

"Natalie has grown children, would you believe. My, how time passes. I haven't heard from her for so many years. I don't know why she chose to call." Mama sounded excited. "She's coming for a visit next week. And when I told her you live near her in Westchester, she said she'd love to see you." I could hear the excitement in Mama's voice. "Why don't you meet her?" Mama asked. The tone of her voice suggested that it was more than a request. "Meet her, she's a doctor and she lives not too far from you. I so loved her mother."

And so Natalie and I met for lunch.

In a small restaurant, with a light breeze from the Hudson in our hair, we revisited our mutual family history, sharing elaborate stories about that immigrant generation of family whose hard transition to life in America we proudly shared.

"Natalie," I said, "I can't tell you how much visiting your parents meant to me. I loved their apartment and the parties they always invited us to. They were so generous with their hospitality and their warm hugs. Mirosha always seemed so much larger than life."

Natalie took a sip of water. "He was. He was."

"And I've always been so impressed with your mother," I continued. "What an elegant woman she was, with her silver hair and her pince-nez. And how amazing that as an immigrant she got to be on the staff of Mount Sinai." I looked at the sunshine reflecting on the Hudson. In my mind, I revisited her family's apartment. I could almost hear Mirosha's booming voice and see Fanny smiling.

"She was so ahead of her time," I said. I felt that I had to make my point about her mother's bravery. "Doing abortions during those years. How amazing was that? And how brave."

The look on Natalie's face shocked me. "You've got to be kidding! Impressed? Amazing? My God, no! I can't believe you thought that."

She stopped eating, put down her fork and sat back. "Do you have any idea what it was like as a child coming back from Dalton at three in the afternoon to find the apartment smelling of ether and worrying that any minute my mother could be arrested and sent to prison? Let me tell you. You think it's so amazing. You've got to be kidding."

"But she was so ... "

She shook her head. "She was so ... what? What it is you think she was? What she was, was jeopardizing me to help strangers." Her face had turned red and I tried to interrupt, to change the subject.

"Natalie, my mother says ..."

But she could not be stopped. "I still can't get over the betrayal of that woman, my mother. Stranger's lives. And what about mine? Her daughter."

I was shocked. "Listen, I'm sorry I started this. I had no way of knowing how you felt. Tell me about your children, your practice. Let's move on to something else." I looked at the speedboat going down the river, trying to restore the sunny afternoon.

NOT PETER

"Peter is going to stay with us during the Easter vacation, while Lucy takes a cruise," my mother said to my father. She came into the living room, where my father was working at his desk. "I just got off the phone with her. A cruise, would you believe?" Lucy, married to my father's brother Miron, was the subject of much family discussion recently. Peter was their only child.

"She asked if I'd mind if he stayed here for the week. She's upset. I think she has called almost every day, telling me all about her and Miron and their problems. So, what could I say? I said 'of course' even though I think she's crazy to even think about throwing Miron out, at this point."

My father looked up from his writing. He put down his pen, took off his glasses and passed a hand through his sparse hair. He smiled at Mama.

"She's going cruising?" he said. "Cruising? Who goes cruising? It's not even warm yet. And may I ask where it is she's cruising to?"

"Who knows," said Mama.

Papa reached for the Lucky Strikes pack and shook one out. He started to put it in his mouth and then returned it. Papa had recently decided to cut down on smoking.

Alex was on his way down the hall. He'd already passed the living room door, but he did a quick about-face and walked back into the room. He was wearing his usual dungarees and Yankee tee shirt. His adored baseball mitt was under his arm, and he was carrying his worn Louisville Slugger bat. At nine, Alex's life revolved around his friends from across the street, on whose team he played *the game* on various baseball diamonds in Riverside Park.

"No dice!" Alex said. "No way! I don't want him here. He's such a pain-in-the neck. That's my vacation, and I don't want him following me around. I'm playing baseball that whole week, and … why does he have to come anyway? He doesn't know my friends, and he's a klutz. He doesn't even want to go to the park. All he likes to do is have me stay home and play games with him. He's ... I don't know. I don't want ... "

From downstairs, through the open window, we heard, "Hey Whitey. Whitey, hey? Ya' coming?" Alex's nickname, engendered by his light skin color and blond hair, was given to him by his Puerto Rican teammates. They were part of the new influx that was changing the neighborhood.

"Go," my mother said to Alex. "Your friends are waiting for you. We'll talk about it later, and I'll explain."

"OK." Alex said. "But maybe," he looked at Mama pleadingly, "Maybe you'll tell me it's a joke."

A look passed between Mama and Papa. I knew it was not a joke.

The previous week we'd been in Great Neck for Passover, at the home of my father's sister Masha and her husband Leo. Although my aunt Masha was the youngest of the four Sokolovsky children that my grandparents, their father and mother, had brought from Odessa in 1917, she was the matriarch of the family. She lived in a large house with a shaded garden full of hostas. Her home was filled with paintings and sculpture. Many of the paintings were her brother Miron's work, and most of the sculptures were hers. She was a gracious hostess, and her home was always open to family and friends.

At least 20 people were sitting around the big maple table in the sunny dining room, including Uncle Leo's sister Edna and her husband. I had ended up sitting at what Masha called the *children's table,* a small card table in the corner, a place where I, 15 years old, felt I did not belong. I tried to turn and participate in the adult conversation, but when one of my younger cousins needed help cutting the meat or pouring milk, I had to help.

At the end of the meal, the younger kids headed down to the basement, but I, determined to establish my adulthood, stayed upstairs. And so I was there when the conversation turned to my Uncle Miron and his wife, Lucy.

"Did he really think he could go off to Mexico to paint, and she'd just be sitting home waiting for him?" Edna asked. She was a small bird-like woman with a high voice. I found her quite irritating.

"She's a hotshot now," she continued. "An important career woman. That silly ditty she wrote, *Three Little Fishes Who Swam and*

Swam, is on the radio all the time." She turned to her husband. "Didn't we just hear it this morning?"

"Yes," he said. "She's a real big deal. And she is not too bad looking either." Edna's expression changed. *Not smart of him,* I thought.

"Well," Aunt Masha said, always ready to defend her younger brother Miron. "I mean, he's *Miron Sokole.* It isn't all *her* who's important, you know. He has a reputation, too. Sharing a studio with Milton Avery and being represented by Midtown Gallery. Museums buy him, for God's sake. Come on." Her voice rose. "He's a star, too." She waved her hand at the many paintings on the dining room wall. There were his abstracts, his realistic pictures from previous Mexico visits, and wonderful oils from his WPA period.

"Yes. He is a star," my father chimed in. "But he's not always the pleasantest star in the constellation. He's his own worst enemy with that sourpuss."

Everyone laughed. I knew that Papa, whose writing skills were not as easily translatable into an American career as his brother's artistic ones, was not Miron's greatest fan.

Masha continued, "We really don't know exactly why he went. He said he was tired of the cold and that he was doing another Mexico series."

She picked up several platters and started toward the kitchen "But six months? Maybe things weren't so good at home, and he headed to Mexico to ease everything. He writes that he's doing good work."

"Maybe he writes to you," my mother said, "but Lucy told me that she hasn't gotten a letter in over a month. Peter got a birthday card, though." Mama got up to help Masha. "I spoke to Lucy just yesterday." The two women were standing in the kitchen doorway, right behind where I was now sitting. Mama said, "She really sounds so unhappy. And would you believe, she told me that she's booked some sort of a cruise. How's that for craziness?"

"What about Peter?" Masha asked.

"Oh, she asked me to take Peter for the week of Easter recess. How can I say no? *Tzuris*—trouble—is *tzuris*, and family is family. I'm going to have lunch at her house on Saturday. Maybe I'll find out what is really going on."

"Well, then call me after," Masha said. "I'll try to get in touch with Miron. Do you think they're thinking of divorcing?"

Wow, I thought. I don't know anyone who is divorced. How exciting! Unlike other women that I knew, who stayed at home and went shopping, Lucy was a career woman, an account executive in an advertising firm. She wore suits with high heels and had elegant leather handbags.

On the subway, going home from Great Neck, I kept replaying the dinner conversation. In my mind, I rooted for Lucy. I liked the feeling of excitement, the feeling that *I* knew someone who would soon be divorced. What an American thing to do!

The following Friday, Alex and I were in the living room. I was trying to win a game of checkers. But we were distracted by Mama's telephone conversation.

"Masha. She *is* going," Mama said. She paused. "Well, yes. I did ask about divorce. She hemmed and hawed. She said she's told Miron that he can't come back to the house when he comes back from Mexico. She's moving all his things to his studio."

Alex and I looked at each other.

I couldn't hear Masha's side of the conversation but she must have asked a question.

"Oh," my mother said. I could hear the smile in her voice. "When I asked her that she said, 'I don't know about divorce. I think I'll just jump overboard instead.'"

Suddenly it occurred to me that maybe this strong American woman, my Aunt Lucy, was not so strong after all.

And then I looked at my brother. He'd overturned the checkerboard, scattering checkers all over the floor. He started out of the room heading toward my mother, still on the hall phone. "It stinks, Mama," he said, pounding his fist into the wall. "She can't jump overboard. She just can't. God, can you imagine. If she jumps overboard, that means we'd have Peter forever!"

RIVA'S STORY

Riva's room was at the end of the hall, right next to the apartment door. She'd lived with us for several years, not quite a roomer, since she was my mother's sister, but not quite a part of our immediate family, since during those years, she and my father were not the best of friends.

He would say to my mother, "Your sister is a *yenta*." His criticism that she couldn't speak correctly in three languages, Yiddish, Russian and English, only now identifies for me that she was dyslexic. I remember that she wrote all her R's backwards. And her name was Riva.

Looking back, I realize that my Aunt Riva must have been a sexy dame. At the time, I thought of her as an old woman, albeit with a wonderful complexion and a great sense of humor. But there was always a man in her life.

Riva and I were sitting at the kitchen table one April evening, drinking tea and visiting, while my parents were at Alex's teacher conference. Riva had been in Florida for several weeks, together with her friend Mr. Friegan. She had come back with a dark tan and lots of stories. Now it was my turn to share.

"Riva, I think I got that assistant counselor's job. I went to an interview yesterday. Would you believe that the interview was in Grand Central terminal, on a wooden bench? But the owner was very nice. He'd come in from somewhere upstate to speak to a few people. He said I'd get a letter about the job. The camp's in the Catskill Mountains, so it should be nice."

"Oh. Good for you. You'll enjoy it. Such a nice way to spend the summer. You'll have a good time." Riva said. "I lived in the Catskill Mountains for many years. I lived in Ellenville, when I was married to Lova. You knew that, right?"

Of course I knew that. "Yes," I said. "Yes. You said you liked it there."

But she seemed bent on telling me a story. I was sure whatever it was I'd heard it already. But I loved Riva's stories. She told them with such wonderful detail. So I took another piece of my mother's raisin babka and sat back to listen.

Riva leaned forward, put her elbows on the table and began.

"Lova and I lived in Ellenville when we got married. Like I told you. Yes?"

I shook my head.

"His soda-water factory was there." I loved the way Riva always said soda-vader-fact-tree. "You've met Lova. Right?"

I'd met Lova many times. But I didn't say that. I just nodded yes.

Lova often visited Papa. They would sit at this kitchen table, laughing and talking. I found him to be different from Papa's other friends. For one thing he wore an eye patch, a black piece of fabric attached to a black string. It covered his left eye, making him look like a pirate—a Jewish one, to be sure.

I knew that he lived in the mountains. Papa told me that Lova hunted and fished and drove a truck. I made up my own stories to explain his patch. I imagined that maybe he'd lost his eye in a hunting accident or had been mauled by a bear. For a New York kid like me, he was a most unforgettable character.

Riva continued. She leaned closer to the table. "We were married about seven or eight years when this happened. I know that I was working, well, not for money, but anyway I was with the Jewish Agency. I think it was Fall, and I remember when I walked up to that cottage ... "

I thought, what cottage? but I didn't want to interrupt. I had never heard this story.

She kept talking. "I heard leaves crunching under my feet. No one had even swept the path to the door. The front step was broken and there was an old icebox on the wooden porch. No bell. So I knocked on the door.

"'Hello,' I said. 'Hello. Anyone home?' I waited but no one answered, and so I knocked again, harder. I heard someone inside. So I started to walk around to the back door. But right then a woman opened the door, dressed in a housedress. Not even all the buttons were closed.

"Lydia. She was so sloppy looking. Her hair was every-which-way. She put her hand on my arm and said, 'Come in—but fast. The baby is on the floor. I'm just warming up her bottle. Hurry 'cause I can't leave her, you know.'"

Riva's lowered her voice. "*Oy*, the terrible Yiddish accent she had. I could hardly understand her."

I couldn't believe that Riva had said that. How funny, I thought, that she didn't know she had an accent, too. Riva took a sip of her tea and continued with her story. She was enjoying having me as her audience.

"So I followed her. We went down this narrow hallway and into the kitchen. And, *Leda*, she never shut her mouth. Talking the whole time. She doesn't even know me, she's telling me her whole life story. Meanwhile, would you believe, there's this tiny baby lying in the center of the floor. Quiet, playing with her feet. The woman hasn't even asked me why I'm there.

"Instead she tells me that she is babysitting and she's only staying for the weekend and that she lives on Delancey Street and took a bus up from New York City yesterday so her daughter could have a day off with her husband. That's how she talked, nonstop. All one long sentence.

"Meanwhile I'm trying to tell her that I'd come from the Jewish Agency to get some forms filled out. That her daughter applied to us for help. Help paying her bills. But I couldn't get one word in. She just keeps talking.

"'*Oy*! How could I not give her a day off?' the woman says. 'She worked in that waitress job until she went to the hospital to have the baby and she worked the whole time since she got married, in the daytime in the restaurant and in the evening helping her husband.'"

"Riva," I interrupted. "Do you want more tea? I'll put more water into the teapot." I started to get up.

"No, *Lydushka*. Thanks. So anyway," Riva continued, "that little woman takes the bottle out of the pot and starts shaking it, still talking. Like nothing stops her. She sits down and sticks the nipple in the baby's mouth. 'Make yourself a potta tea,' she told me, like I belonged in that house. Really, I think she wasn't all right in the head. She wouldn't let me get a word in. She was feeding the little baby and talking like she had no one to talk to for years. I tell you it's no wonder that she lived on Delancey Street and her daughter moved to Ellenville.

"'So mine daughter gets a job in a hotel, waiting on the customers. I tell you she is such a hard-working girl and beautiful, not old like me. And then,' the woman continues, 'God smiles on her. A man who works here in town falls in love with her. So they came to New York City Hall to get married. They didn't have to get married in New York, you know. They did it for Moshe and me. I think that was the happiest day in mine life.'"

Riva looked at me. "So, quite a story already, right?" Actually, I was tired of sitting there. I wanted to call my friend Ros and make plans for Saturday. But I knew that Riva had more to say.

"So this old woman, she's burping the baby and talking without stopping. I tried to interrupt her. I wanted to leave. 'When do you expect her?' I asked. 'Why don't I just leave my papers and come back when they come home?'

"'*Oy*,' the lady said. 'She is coming back tonight, but her husband, *oy*, he works so hard. Always traveling. He travels so much. Such a wonderful man even if he does not make such a good living. A beautiful person. Sometimes he is away for four or five days at a time. He takes his car, and he drives all over the Catskills. What a way to make a living. And with money so hard. He says the rooming houses he has to sleep in are not always so nice. And to drive at night. On these roads. Not so wonderful. Right?'"

Riva looked at me. "Such a good man," she said sarcastically. She continued her story.

"'Please. I'll come back,' I told the lady, 'Lady. I will come here tomorrow. I can leave the papers with you.'"

Riva took a sip of tea. But she wasn't finished with her story. I wondered when Mama, Papa and Alex would be home.

Riva went on. "The little woman finished giving the baby the bottle. She stood up and put the little girl in the bassinet. It looked not so new, that bassinet.

"'*Oy*,' the woman started kvetching again. 'OK. I walk you to the door,' she says. But she still wouldn't shut up. 'You know he owns a factory here in town that makes seltzer and sodavater. Honestly, when I first met him I thought he wasn't such a catch. But you know he is so nice to me and to mine daughter.'

"I had the door open," Riva said.

"'I'll be back to pick up the papers on Friday,' I told her. But she kept on talking, that little woman.

"'So he only has one eye. So. No one's perfect, you know. And he's such a real Yankee. He hunts and shoots. Only he shot out his eye and now he wears a black patch over it,' she says."

Riva's eyes glistened. She looked at me. Wow, I thought. She's talking about Lova! No wonder she's divorced. My God. What a story. Now I knew why Mama always went out when Lova came. Why she didn't like it when Papa had him to the house.

I looked at my aunt. I didn't know what to say. "Riva," I said. "Maybe you want some more tea ... or something?"

LIVES LIVED

"Hold on," says the woman at the cemetery where my uncle Misha is buried. "I'll be right back to you with that information. We don't get such requests too often, but I do know that there are some forms to be filled out. And the State has laws that have to be followed. Can you hold on for a few minutes? I'm downstairs and I have to get back to my desk. OK?"

I'm sitting at my kitchen table. My Aunt Riva's funeral was over a week ago, and I miss her terribly. I look out of the window at my backyard with the swing set that Riva and Misha had given us. The sun is shimmering on the young green leaves and my mind wanders to another day, another time, other trees, many years ago.

Louise and I were cutting our fourth period class at Hunter College.

"Where is your uncle's place, anyway?" Louise stepped around the grate in the sidewalk. "I hate walking on those. They give me the creeps ever since I saw the story in the *Daily News* about the guy who fell through."

I moved over to give her room.

"It's wonderful being out of school, walking." Louise kept talking. "How nice to think that winter is finally over. It's so gorgeous out. Really warm. I could have worn my spring topper, not this blah winter coat. Actually, really, maybe we shouldn't come back after."

"Humm, that's so tempting, not coming back. We just have a few more weeks. Let's see if it's still so nice after we pick up that package at Misha's place."

"How far is it?"

"On 82nd Street between 2nd and 3rd. Wait till you meet him. He's like a hero from Joseph Conrad's novels. He has the coolest stuff. My father is making a bookcase, and Misha has some fancy hardware to give him. Misha is really one interesting guy."

"I've heard so much about him. He's the one who's married to your aunt Riva, right. Do they have children?

"Not together, this is his second marriage. First, he was married to my cousin Betty, the ophthalmologist. And when she died, I guess he wanted to stay in the family. He's not Jewish, you know, but he's not religious at all. So after Betty died he asked my mother's sister, my aunt Riva, to marry him. Funny, she went from Jalkow, a Jewish name, to Andronoff, really Russian. And she uses it. She is now Riva Andronoff. Betty, his first wife, always used her own name, even though they were married for such a long time."

"Maybe that was because she was a doctor, don't you think? How'd a doctor marry a plumber anyway?"

Louise and I had been friends for only about six months, since the start of Hunter. I had been to her house a few times. And although she'd not yet been to mine, we shared family stories.

"Well," I said, answering her question, "Misha wasn't always a plumber." I dodged a small dog trying to pull his owner toward the curb.

"He was an engineering cadet at a military academy in Turkistan. He must have been really handsome in his uniform, 'cause he's still nice looking. Wait 'til you meet him. Very Russian. And when the Revolution started, both the White Army and the Red Army wanted to enlist him. So he ran north, between their lines." I'd heard the story of his journey so many times. And then, I don't get the geography from there, he ended up in Shanghai."

"No kidding. He did that by himself?"

I put my hand out to keep Louise from crossing in front of a kid on roller skates. "Watch where you're going!" I yelled at him.

"I don't know how he got there. But he met my aunt Betty in Shanghai, and I think they got married there. They came to the States together."

We turned the corner of Lexington and 82nd Street. And there was the sign, "Yorkville Plumbing." It hung above the steps leading down to Misha's basement shop. The brownstone, which he owned, looked like all the others in this German section of New York, Yorkville.

We could hear him from the street. His English was perfect, his Russian accent charming. "*God-damn-shit.* No, I said I wouldn't do that job for her. Go back and tell that woman that after the way she treated you, I will not let you work in her damn, dirty apartment." Although I couldn't see him, Misha must have been talking to Steven, his apprentice.

God-damn-shit was Misha's favorite expression. He used it for both pleasure and anger. Every weekend, on the way to whatever grassy picnic area he'd picked out in upstate New York or across the river in New Jersey, we heard a constant chorus of *God-damn-shit*s. The driver in front was going too slowly. *God-damn-shit*. Not staying in his lane, *God-damn-shit*. The food was especially tasty. *God-damn-shit, this is good.*

Misha and Riva would spend the week preparing salads and marinating lamb with spices, lemon, and onion, for entertaining the family on weekends. Misha's steel-drum grill, made in his plumbing shop, and his constantly refilled glass of Seagrams-7 were staples in our family life. Riva, meticulous as always, brought folded napkins, plates, a tablecloth, and the bread. We (my father, mother, brother, myself, and whatever cousins lived in the selected area), as the invited guests, were forbidden to contribute to the meal.

When Louise and I walked in the door, Misha, hands black as always from pipes and solder, came toward us. "Look at that. What the day brought in. Hello, hello. Too nice for school, no? Not good. You need to be educated. Look at me, a plumber. *God-damn-shit*. You don't want that."

But I knew that regret was not really part of his vocabulary.

"No, don't worry. You're already in college. A nice day off won't hurt you. Not so bad." He walked to the back of the long shop and got a paper bag. "Here, give this to Abram. And tell Rosa that we're driving to Morristown this Saturday. Iz and Helga will meet us there. Oh," Misha walked to the counter near the door, "Take this cake for you two. It's *kolisch*, Russian Easter Bread."

I loved Russian Easter food. The colored eggs, the *paska*, made from strained cottage cheese and candied fruits, and best of all the *kolisch*, yeast dough baked in a can for a risen brown dome. Ever since my days in a Russian nursery school and kindergarten, I relished the Russian Orthodox celebration, ceremonies, and food. And with Misha in the family, we enjoyed the combination of both Jewish and Russian Orthodox people and foods.

When we left his shop, we walked up 82nd Street into Central Park, munching our cake and talking. We talked about how religion separates people, and how wonderful my Aunt Riva and Uncle Misha were together. What fun they had enjoying each other's holidays, and what joy they brought to our family. We never did return to our last class.

It was still warm out. The young leaves of an early spring shone in the sun. We sat on a park bench and, as college students tend to do, we engaged in long philosophical discussions. About God, man, about worship, and how families are created. And what makes for love.

Five years later, when Misha died, I helped my Aunt Riva make burial arrangements for him. I called my friend Louise. "I needed to tell this to someone," I said. "I am outraged. Would you believe that the Jewish section of the IWO cemetery in Long Island, where Riva had bought two plots, would not allow Misha to be buried there?"

"I don't blame you. Of all people, your Uncle Misha. He just wasn't due such treatment." Louise sounded as upset as I was.

"I'm just seething," I continued. "The small-mindedness of religion. This should never have affected Misha. Really. Not him. What is religion all about anyway? Keeping people out?"

And so, Misha's funeral was held in New Jersey, in a plot, newly purchased, where he was buried far from our family or from anyone he knew.

Riva lived for another 12 years. Then, finally, she was laid to rest in the cemetery in Long Island where she'd hoped to lie with Misha.

"Hello, are you still there?" The voice on the telephone interrupts my long daydream. "Well, it turns out that it is no problem transferring Misha Adronoff's body to that other cemetery. We could probably do it next week if we get all the papers filled out. I'll call you tomorrow with the cost and exact date."

I call the IWO cemetery on Long Island to tell them to expect my Misha's body. No questions are asked. And so none are answered.

I hang up the phone.

I sit back. And then I hear Misha. He's laughing.

"That was a good one, right, Misha?" I think.

And I hear a loud, clear voice saying "*God-damn-shit!*"

OUR PROFESSORS

"I'll carry it," Claire said picking up the table. "You run interference, babe. God, I hope we can carry this thing into the elevator. Lydia, stay ahead of me. OK?" She laughed, "What a joke. Getting this thing upstairs."

I pushed out my elbows, trying to make my body wider so that I could part the crowd. "Hey, coming through, coming through," I kept saying. Jelly was carrying the large poster with *Don't Whitewash McCarthy; Impeach Him* printed on it in large yellow and black letters. I was carrying the yellow flyers and cakes of soap wrapped in mailing envelopes, to be sent to New York State legislators.

"That was really stupid, to do it now. Carry a card table upstairs. Couldn't ya' have waited just 20 minutes? It's change time. I told you to wait." Jelly, round and redheaded, always thought she knew best. "I can hardly get down the halls at two-forty anyway. Just forget trying to get a table through." Jelly was fun when she wasn't being bossy.

Claire had asked Agnes, a freshman student council delegate, to meet us at the end of the seventh floor corridor, help us set up the table and then sit there, collecting contributions for the *Impeach campaign*, but we were still on the third floor. It was just five minutes 'til the start of the next class, and students were rushing in both directions, trying to avoid the usual scrutiny of entering a class after a professor had started taking attendance.

Change of class at Hunter was a period of intense activity, the wrong time to bring a card table anywhere, but we needed to be done with it. Dean Trinsey's monthly Student-Faculty tea was at three. And no one came late to *this* Dean's office. Her sterling manners and British accent were meant to set the example for those of us who were not used to sitting with our legs crossed at the ankles, balancing cups of tea in our laps while carrying on polite conversation.

"Hunter girls are to be exemplary young women as well as good students," she preached. "They must be able to conduct themselves in all situations."

Jelly looked unhappily at Claire. "I've got it, Jelly. Don't worry, for Christ's sake. I can handle it." Claire said. Claire could handle anything: a basketball, an out-of-line Student Council Member. Even Professor Stevenson, who liked the blonde girls better than brunettes, or at least that was what we all thought. President of the Hunter College Student Council, dark-haired Claire was admired for her judicial skills and her superb figure.

She juggled the table against her hip, her plaid skirt bunching up slightly. The hall behind us was crowded with students moving to their next class.

"And after that stupid idea you had during lunch hour," Jelly, her long red hair swinging, breathlessly hurried behind us. "To go across the street to see the inside of that Russian consulate. Jeez."

"Ah, come' on, babe," Claire called everyone *babe*. "I've always wanted to see the inside. Here we've spent years looking at that marble building, with those guards outside. And boy, they'd stare me down when I'd say *hi*.

"But today, with Vyshinsky dying and all those people standing in line to view the body, I thought, 'Hey, why not us?' And it worked." She held on to the table and punched the elevator button again. "We got in, right? Tell me you didn't think it was pretty neat inside. Huh, babe? All that marble and shiny glass, and that fat Vyshinsky in that satin lined coffin. See, I take you to the best places."

"Ya, but Claire. I told you, while we were waiting in line, there were those men, looked like Feebs. Not press. These guys were standing there on the curb, photographing us. They were flashing those bulbs right into our faces. Everyone's faces. And they weren't even trying to hide it." I couldn't erase the uneasy feeling I had had. "Probably now we all have FBI files. They have our pictures, outside with all those Russians."

"Ah, come on. Let's not get paranoid now. We weren't the only curious tourists, babe. And anyway, who cares?" Claire said.

Sure, I thought. She doesn't care. Her parents were born here, not like mine. "Here. Hold that door," I said. Finally we were in the elevator.

"Let's make some room, ladies. Push in!" Claire pushed toward the back, squeezing two girls into a corner, smiling all the while. Jelly and I crowded in behind her.

"Sorry," I said to the girl whose toe I'd stepped on.

"But it was gorgeous inside," Jelly continued talking. "Those Russians sure know how to live. Did you see them? Ugly men in black suits in that great house. Just standing there while the people walked in, in line." She held her books away from the elevator door. "All that marble, and the crystal chandeliers. God, everyone waiting in line to see a dead body. I can't believe it. And now this disaster. But I think we're OK. We'll be on time."

Several weeks before that, at a Student Council Meeting, class representatives had discussed the happenings at the various City Colleges and what we, as students, could do about them. I had attended the meeting as Vice-President of the Junior Class. Everyone was talking about the three Hunter professors who had been fired by the Board of Higher Education. Then someone brought up how the Board had closed the student newspapers at Brooklyn and City College and threatened to expel the editors. Another student proposed that the Council contribute money to create a legal defense fund for our professors.

We had a heated discussion about this. Some Student Council members felt we should mind our own business. Others insisted that since the professors knew that the City Council had interpreted the Feinberg Law to mean that refusing to answer a Congressional Committee's questions would lead to immediate dismissal, it was their own fault that they were let go. I didn't know Louis Weisner or Charles Hughes, but I'd had Jerauld McGill for philosophy and couldn't believe that such a quiet shy man could be a threat to anyone. He'd once taught at Harvard, and was so gentlemanly toward his students. Discussion continued long after the usual five o'clock deadline.

The issue of raising money to help these professors obtain legal representation kept us at the Council arguing late into the evening. Finally, we agreed that we shouldn't pledge Student Council funds, since there were students who felt that these professors should indeed have been fired. Hunter College President George Shuster then said we could set up tables and collect money from those students who wanted to contribute. Jelly came up with the idea of selling soap to mail to our State legislators. And another delegate suggested that we put up a sign protesting the *"whitewash."*

We set up the table at the end of the hall, and left. Agnes was putting out the flyers and soap. Some curious students were already crowding around.

"Claire," I asked as we were climbing the two flights to Dean Trinsey's office, "Are you going to bring up Friday night's play?" Friday night had been the opening performance of the Drama Club's *The Crucible*, Arthur Miller's play about the Salem witch-hunts. "I mean, it was really weird seeing Dean Trinsey and President Shuster there in the front row. Don't you think?"

Jelly was taking the steps two at a time. She stopped and turned around. "Why? Why was it weird? I mean, they've been at every other opening. Why shouldn't they be at this one?"

"Well, ah," I stopped also. Claire, two steps behind, caught up, and the three of us sat down. I put my books down behind me. We often had mini-meetings in the stairwell. It was quiet and private. "I guess we shouldn't sit too long. We'll be late for tea."

"Yeah," Claire laughed. "Just like the white rabbit. You know, actually, sometimes when we're there with our cookies and tea, I feel just like Alice in Wonderland. Don't you, babe?"

"Oh, I don't know." I leaned back against the green wall. "We drink tea at home, too. But not with milk. And I don't have to balance the cup in my lap. But really, it was weird wasn't it? I mean the play. About witch hunts. And we're having one at Hunter. I kind'a thought that maybe the top administrators wouldn't be there, what with the Board looking into everyone's life. Like maybe our College witch hunt would … "

"Hunter isn't so bad," Jelly interrupted. "I mean, it's not like Brooklyn and City where they made the student editors of their newspapers resign. They threatened them with being thrown out of school if they made a fuss.

"And we've got Shuster. He's in with the Catholic Church. And Cavallero, the chairman, and the rest of those morons at the Board of Higher Ed, are afraid of his influence. Jeez, he's such a scholar he could walk circles around those fools. They sure wouldn't take him on. He's friends with the Cardinal and all. And anyway, he's really a special man."

"Ya," Claire moved her legs so that a girl going up the stairs could get by us. "But wasn't it terrible when the lights came on, to turn around and see those three professors right behind us? It was like they were watching their own lives. Those people in Salem getting hysterical and seeing witches everywhere. And turning on their friends. I couldn't believe the three of them would be there. It was terrible."

"Ya," I said. "I turned around when you poked me. But I didn't want them to think I was looking at them, so I just looked back, like at the doors. And then I pretended I didn't see that McGill had tears in his eyes."

"Ya. Me too," said Jelly.

"Me too, babe, me too," said Claire. "I sure didn't want them to think I was looking at them."

We got up, straightened our skirts, and continued up the stairs to Dean's Trinsey's very civilized tea.

SECRETS

Papa always said, "What goes on in this house, stays in this house."

With Papa, it was always stories. Some were larger than life, others life itself. His life. The life he lived and the life he dreamed. Telling on him now evokes in me a terrible sense of betrayal. I was never supposed to reveal so many of the things I knew. In some ways, this is just the way people lived back then, keeping family matters private. But as I came to understand, many of the things that should "stay in the house" concerned justifiable fears of the world around them, some of which I knew and others that I can now only guess at. We celebrated Papa's birthday on May 1st. Ask the young me when my father was born, and I would say five-one-ninety-nine, May 1st, 1899. I would say that his birthday ushered in spring. That it revealed a taste of summer soon to come.

I can see him now walking amidst the budding cherry trees on the Riverside Drive bike path. He is dressed in dark blue slacks, a black shirt and black tie. A tweed jacket is hanging on his index finger, jauntily slung over his shoulder. On his head he wears a straw boater. He is never hatless. In summer, he wears straw. Sometimes his summer hat is small-brimmed. But on especially sunny days, he has on his head a farmer's hat, straw, with wide turned up edges.

In winter, of course, he wore black felt. I can see him in our kitchen, steaming his hat over a pot of boiling water, then carefully pushing the nap in one direction with the boar-bristled brush.

But May 1st was not only his birthday, it was, coincidentally, May Day. A maypole kind of day, when spring awakens and children put flowers in their hair. A day when Labor worldwide celebrates solidarity, the day that the Left has always considered its own. And it is, as well, the feast day of Saint John the Worker, although I always wondered if that mattered.

We (Papa and Mama, and therefore Alex and I as well) were a Labor family. We never crossed a picket line, and we believed that the bosses, whoever they were, took advantage of all working people. In all organized labor causes, we rallied. So with Papa's birthday on May 1st, we had many reasons to celebrate.

Papa wasn't always a union worker. He'd worked for the City Welfare Department until the Civil Service Act had mandated compulsory courses be taken, and Papa made other choices. Now he stood on his feet, eight hours a day, in a factory located on 32nd Street. When I was about fifteen, he invited me to come see what he did to earn a living. And also (I knew this even then) to show me off, his American pride and joy, to, as he would say, "the scum he worked with."

Of course, I knew that I couldn't tell anyone what Papa did for a living. I'm still uncomfortable revealing it. Where it said *father's occupation* on any form I had to fill out, I wrote "salesman." Such were my instructions. And when people asked me (although in those days it was not considered a polite question), I told them the same thing.

My friend Louise had confided in me that her father was a housepainter.

"Would you believe he wears a suit and tie when he goes to work?" she said, her American disdain for occupational prejudices evident. She said he did not want his neighbors to know that he was a laboring man and not the violinist that he had been in Poland. "He feels so demeaned," she said. I never told her that my father, too, felt demeaned by his job. I never told her what Papa did for a living.

On the day that I went to visit my father's place of work, I took the subway downtown and walked to 32nd Street. I headed past rusty iron gates that led to loading docks, past crumpled newspapers blown up against wire mesh garbage cans, past the men pushing racks of clothes and hand trucks filled with cardboard boxes. I kept looking at the building numbers until I found the one Papa had given me, opened a metal door and walked into the narrow hallway.

The elevator was operated by a small black man.

"What floor, miss?"

"Modern Pocketbooks. What floor is that?" I asked.

"You're going to six."

When the iron gates of the industrial elevator closed and it began its creaky ascent past other factory floors, I glanced at the cement walls, marked with years of grime, and wanted to leave. But I was expected. And then the elevator shook to a stop.

"Here you are, honey." The elevator man pulled back the gate, and I walked into a world of noise, men standing at long tables, glue pots, and brushes, amidst an assortment of leather and knives.

I saw Papa heading in my direction. He put his arm around me and walked me into the office, a windowed cubicle in the corner near the elevator door. "This is my daughter, Lydia," he said to a short bald man, whom I recognized. "And this is Mr. Mutterpearl, the owner of Modern Pocketbooks."

I smiled.

"Hello, my dear," said the man, obviously not recognizing me. "You have a wonderful father." He looked like he wanted us out of his way.

"You have a lovely daughter, Abe. What grade are you in, dear?"

"High School," I answered.

Papa put his hand on my elbow and guided me out toward one of the long tables. "This is Juan, and this is Pierre," he said. Papa looked different from many of his co-workers, I thought, although I did spot some lighter skinned people at the tables.

He took me around, his hand on my elbow, helping me maneuver around workers gluing leather to fabric, around the boxes piled on lint-covered floors, and introduced me.

"This is my daughter," he said. I smiled and uttered *hello*, and we moved on, across to another table where people were using sharp knives to cut brightly colored leather around paper patterns.

Then he guided me toward the elevator and pushed the button. I'd been there all of 10 minutes.

"I'm glad you came. This was something you needed to see. How I make a living. But this is no place for you. Go enjoy yourself." He put his hand into his pocket and took out some money. "Go to Gimbels, and buy yourself something nice. And there's a *Chock Full of Nuts* on 34th Street. Get that cream cheese sandwich that you like so much." He gave me a hug. "I'll see you at home. This is not the place for you."

"Thanks, Papa," I said. "But I have something to tell you. Quietly."
I leaned toward him. "You know that man in the office, the first one
I met? I know him, Papa."

Papa looked at me. "Mr. Mutterpearl? How do you know him?
He's the owner of this place. How do you know him?" He asked
again. "You know Mutterpearl?"

"Papa. I know him from Temple Ansche Chesed." That was
the Temple on 100th Street, where I played ping-pong on weekends
and where my *B'nai Brith Girls* group met. "He comes down to the
gym lots of times to see what we are up to. He's the president of the
congregation. He always wears a hat, and he struts around and pats
everyone on the head." I tried to see him through the window of
his office, but he wasn't there anymore. "Everyone looks up to him."

Papa smiled. "Yes. I heard he was an important man in the
Jewish community. Word gets around. But that bastard is the worst
sweatshop owner there is. The Union is always fighting with him.
He has no respect for working people."

"Really?" I couldn't imagine that this was the same Mr. Mutterpearl that seemed so nice when I saw him at the Temple.

"Really," said Papa. "He just fired Mary McGinnis, his secretary,
when she came in late because she had to take her daughter to the
hospital."

The secret of Papa's occupation is still with me, but seems extra-
neous to all that was my father. For all of his political idealism and the
real risks people like my parents took, he disparaged the uneducated
men with whom he had to work. That was not his vision of himself.

After all of these years, I still see my father the way he saw himself—proud, good-looking and dapper, with a Talmudic mind and
intellectual interests, not a slave earning a living in what for him was
an unsavory way.

Yet he was also an immigrant and a man of the Left, although
he gradually lost his certainty and his ardor faded as union leaders
got fat and Stalin's empire assassinated Jews under the Iron Curtain.
And, of course, I remember him as a dreamer.

So when, after his death, I came across his citizenship applica-
tion, I was surprised and amused to see a different birthday, his real
birthday, July 27. The May Day birthday was an invention symbol-
izing his early belief in the sanctity of labor and chosen when he still

believed in a bright and promising future. July 27th, up until then, had been important to me only because it is the day that my grandson was born. But it was *Bam's* birthday, too. I loved it.

ABOUT THE AUTHOR

Dr. Lydia S. Rosner, Professor Emeritus of Sociology, has been on the faculty at John Jay College of Criminal Justice, City University of New York since 1985. Her expertise includes system beating behavior, migration and crime and bureaucratic structures. She has published extensively in newspapers, including *The New York Times,* and in professional journals and authored *The Soviet Way of Crime: Beating the System in the Soviet Union and the USA*. She served as Project Director at the National Center for Public Productivity and Assistant Director of Research at the Criminal Justice Center at John Jay College.

Mentioned in *Two Thousand Notable American Women, Who's Who in America* and *Who's Who in the East*, Dr. Rosner has traveled the world with a keen interest in cultures and social structures. Having long-standing family ties to Western Massachusetts, she has become an active member of the Board of the Berkshire Museum. She is currently at work on a family history project.

She is particularly thankful to her late husband, Jonathan L Rosner, for 52 years of happiness, and proud of her wonderful children and grandchildren.

OTHER RECENT TITLES FROM MAYAPPLE PRESS:

John Palen, *Small Economies,* 2012
        Paper, 58pp, $13.95 plus s&h
        ISBN 978-1-936419-09-8
Susan Azar Porterfield, *Kibbe,* 2012
        Paper, 62pp, $14.95 plus s&h
        ISBN 978-1-936419-08-1
Susan Kolodny, *After the Firestorm,* 2011
        Paper, 62pp, $14.95 plus s&h
        ISBN 978-1-936419-07-4
Eleanor Lerman, *Janet Planet*, 2011
        Paper, 210pp, $16.95 plus s&h
        ISBN 978-1-936419-06-7
George Dila, *Nothing More to Tell*, 2011
        Paper, 100pp, $15.95 plus s&h
        ISBN 978-1-936419-05-0
Sophia Rivkin, *Naked Woman Listening at the Keyhole*, 2011
        Paper, 44pp, $13.95 plus s&h
        ISBN 978-1-936419-04-3
Stacie Leatherman, *Stranger Air*, 2011
        Paper, 80pp, $14.95 plus s&h
        ISBN 978-1-936419-03-6
Mary Winegarden, *The Translator's Sister*, 2011
        Paper, 86pp, $14.95 plus s&h
        ISBN 978-1-936419-02-9
Howard Schwartz, *Breathing in the Dark*, 2011
        Paper, 96pp, $15.95 (hardcover $24.95) plus s&h
        ISBN 978-1-936419-00-5 (hc 978-1-936419-01-2)
Paul Dickey, *They Say This Is How Death Came into the World*, 2011
        Paper, 78 pp, $14.95 plus s&h
        ISBN 978-0932412-997
Sally Rosen Kindred, *No Eden*, 2011
        Paper, 70 pp, $14.95 plus s&h
        ISBN 978-0932412-980
Jane O. Wayne, *The Other Place You Live*, 2010
        Paper, 80 pp, $14.95 plus s&h
        ISBN 978-0932412-973

For a complete catalog of Mayapple Press publications, please visit our website at *www.mayapplepress.com*. Books can be ordered direct from our website with secure on-line payment using PayPal, or by mail (check or money order). Or order through your local bookseller.